Healthcare Staffing & Budgeting
Practical Management Tools

Roey Kirk, M.S.M.

AN ASPEN PUBLICATION®
Aspen Publishers, Inc.

1988

Rockville, Maryland
Royal Tunbridge Wells

Library of Congress Cataloging-in-Publication Data

Kirk, Roey.
Healthcare staffing & budgeting: practical management tools/Roey Kirk.
p. cm.
"An Aspen publication."
ISBN: 0-87189-784-9
1. Health facilities--Business management--Handbooks, manuals, etc.
2. Health facilities--Business management--Forms. 3. Health facilities--Personnel
management--Handbooks, manuals, etc. 4. Health facilities--Personnel
management--Forms. I. Title. II. Title: Healthcare staffing and budgeting.
[DNLM: 1. Health Facilities--economics--United States. 2. Personnel Administration,
Hospital--economics--United States. 3. Personnel Administration,
Hospital--organization & administration. 4. Personnel Management--manpower--United States.
WX 159 K588h]
RA971.3.K57   1988   362.1′068--dc19   DNLM/DLC
for Library of Congress
88-6184
CIP

Aspen Publishers, Inc. grants permission for photocopying for personal, internal, and limited
business purposes. This consent does not extend to other kinds of copying, such as copying for
general distribution, for advertising or promotional purposes, for creating new works, or for resale.
For information address Aspen Publishers, Inc.
1600 Research Boulevard, Rockville, Maryland 20850.

Library of Congress Catalog Card Number: 88-6184
ISBN: 0-87189-784-9

Printed in the United States of America

1 2 3 4 5

Table of Contents

Preface vii

Section 1:
Developing the Unit of Service and
Identifying the Department's Standard 1

    Introduction: Getting Started 1
    Service Units 2
    Assigning Time Values to Service Units 3
    Supportive Information to Gather 4
    Determining Standards 5
    Logging and Documenting Activities 6
    Activity Time Log (Form 1.1-Example) 7
    Activity Time Log (Form 1.1) 8
    Benefits of an Accurately Defined Service Unit 11

Section 2:
Using Patient Care & Service Standards for Budget Planning 13

    Ensuring a Preselected Level of Quality 13
    Applications of Standard Time Values 15
    Using Standard Time Values to Calculate Your Department's
        Hours per Modality (HPM) 16
    Calculating Standards Using Retrospective Classification Data (Form 2.1-Examples) .. 16
    Calculating Standards (Form 2.1) 20
    Average Volume & Average Acuity - Why Are They Important? 21
    What If the Calculated Standard Is Not Approved? 22

Section 3:
Using Patient Care & Service Standards for Budget Calculation 25

    The Budget Process 25
    Calculating FTE Required for a Desired Level of Quality 26
    Volume 28
    Flexible (Direct) FTE 29
    Fixed FTE 30

Nonproductive FTE 31
Total Adjusted FTE 32
Adjusted Care Hours per Modality (HPM) 32
Acuity- & Volume-based Staffing Budget 33
Acuity- & Volume-based Staffing Budget (Form 3.1-Example) 34
Acuity- & Volume-based Staffing Budget (Form 3.1) 35

Section 4:
Staffing Pattern Development 37

Using Standard Hours per Modality 37
Preparing Data for the Staffing Pattern 38
Staffing Pattern Information 40
Creating the Daily Staffing Pattern 44
Staffing Pattern (Form 4.1-Example) 47
Staffing Pattern (Form 4.1) 48
Staffing Pattern Variation (Form 4.2) 49

Section 5:
Prospective Budget Control 51

Planning Ahead for "On Target" Performance 51
External and Internal Variables 53
Position Control 54
Position Control (Form 5.1) 55
Position Control (Form 5.1-Example) 56
Footnotes: Position Control (Form 5.1-Example) 57
Performance Appraisal Systems: Personnel's Role in Prospective Budget Control ...58
Job Standards Provide Prospective and Ongoing Budget Control 59
Prehiring Agreements 59
Prehire Agreement & Documentation (Form 5.2-Example) 63
Prehire Agreement & Documentation (Form 5.2) 64

Section 6:
Prescheduling Staff: More Planning Ahead 67

Prescheduling - The Last Plan 67
Preplanning, Preparation, Process 69
Vacation Notice (Form 6.1) 72
Vacation Memo (Form 6.2) 73
Request for Days Off (Form 6.3) 74
Policy Issues: Requests for Days Off 75

Vacation Schedule (Form 6.4-Example) 76
Vacation Schedule (Form 6.4) 77
Basic Scheduling Techniques...78
Vacation Approval (Form 6.5) 79
The Scheduling Process, Step-by-Step 80
Priorities and Scheduling 83
Scheduling Exercise 84
Daily Schedule (Form 6.6-Exercise) 85
Daily Schedule (Form 6.6-Exercise Answer & Example) 86
Daily Schedule (Form 6.6) 87

Section 7:
Making Schedules Flexible 89

Scheduling as a Recruitment & Retention Tool 89
Assessing Satisfaction Levels 90
Satisfaction Questionnaire (Form 7.1) 91
Evaluating Flexible Scheduling Plans 93
Glossary: Flexible Scheduling Options 94
Traditional Schedules 96
12-Hour Shift Schedules 98
12-Hour Weekend Schedules 100
Justifying Flexible Scheduling 102
Implementation Strategy 104

Preface

Competency and responsibility levels continue to evolve for healthcare managers, growing to new levels of sophistication in a dynamic and constantly changing healthcare industry. With each change and new development, healthcare managers who choose to maintain their position and level of involvement grow as well. Granted, there are occasional growing pains, but sharpened skills, new information sources, and a wealth of different experiences are positive payoffs that have catapulted many healthcare managers to levels of managerial competency they may have never thought possible.

Being a competent manager in today's healthcare industry is more complex and much more demanding than it was ten years ago. As a result, today's practicing managers are hungry for knowledge relating to every aspect of their department. There is an increasing awareness that the best way to optimize patient care while maximizing financial and competitive outcomes is to manage all aspects of the department. Many are seeking, or being offered, more authority over many entities for which they've always had some element of responsibility and accountability. With the new control comes the need for back-up systems, methods, and management tools to facilitate effective, efficient decision making.

The purpose of this book is to provide these back-up systems, methods, and techniques for managers and administrators to help them manage their units, departments, and divisions more effectively and more efficiently with the indirect but ultimate focus on improving patient care and related services. The book is filled with practical management tools that have been used successfully and taught to hundreds of students, managers, and administrators. This book doesn't just tell you how you should do things, it provides forms and formulas that can be copied and implemented immediately. The goal is not to tie up your time recreating an idea from the book, but rather to give you the opportunity to quickly try an idea and assess its potential application in your organization.

The step-by-step instruction style enables both independent and classroom learning. Practicing healthcare managers and administrators will find this an excellent resource for new ideas, innovations, and challenges that will help them manage their responsibilities. In addition, key concepts, formulas, and forms have been set up so that educators of healthcare management and administration students can make overhead transparencies and homework assignments directly from the book examples. Each form and worksheet is set up two ways: (1) The first presentation is an example, which is filled in to show how it is used; (2) The second presentation, which follows, is a blank form ready for copying. For those of you who want to revise or personalize the forms, they are available in software format, compatible with Apple's Macintosh™ hardware, from the author (Roey Kirk Associates, P.O. Box 160309, Miami, FL 33116).

Although the outline of the book follows a process that is best understood when read in order, the text has also been designed to meet the needs of readers who only want to read a particular section. In Section 1, Developing the Unit of Service and Identifying the Department's Standard, the process begins by looking at the department's unit of service—the modality—as the key factor in managing staffing and budgeting responsibilities. Drawing on the expertise of the staff, the unit of service can be evaluated to identify the average amount of care hours required per patient modality or related service.

Once the standard number of care hours per patient modality is established, it can be used as baseline data for upcoming fiscal year budget activities. Sections 2 and 3, Using Patient Care & Service Standards for Budget Planning and Calculation, describe ways to plan and prepare for: (1) budget calculation activities, (2) ongoing quality and productivity monitoring, and (3) unexpected variations in both volume and acuity. In Section 4, Staffing Pattern Development, the same unit standard is used to outline a plan for prescheduling staff in a consistent, flexible pattern designed to meet both the needs of the patient and the cost containment goals of the institution.

Section 5, Prospective Budget Control, addresses a variety of internal and external variables that affect budget performance. Although many of these variables are beyond the control of the department manager, outcomes can be influenced by taking a proactive stance by planning ahead through the use of position control, performance management systems, and prehiring agreements. Section 6, Prescheduling Staff: More Planning Ahead, scheduling techniques are demonstrated, showing how to preschedule staff with predictable quality and financial results. When staff are prescheduled according to the identified standard number of care hours per patient modality, the manager achieves maximum flexibility in meeting patient care needs by adjusting staff to match daily fluctuations in volume and acuity. Section 7, Making Schedules Flexible, builds on basic scheduling techniques, and shows how to use this important function for the purpose of recruiting and retaining employees to fill budgeted positions.

Years ago when I prepared the budgets and schedules for five critical care nursing departments, staff members were always coming and going from my office. If they weren't negotiating for time off or volunteering to work extra, they were picking up their earned bag of M & Ms™ for saving my life by working a double shift. Occasionally they would leave with this parting remark: "I wouldn't have your job for all the money in the world." My chin dropped lower and lower. One day I got smart. I realized staffing didn't have to be that way, at least not all the time. I listened to the nurses who were telling me about quality and staffing being more than numbers, and it changed the way I managed—forever. I realized that quality had to be defined before it could be quantified. Once it was quantified, it could be used for managing the departmental budget activities, productivity results, scheduling practices, and even employee performance. I carried this philosophy over to several other departments outside nursing and to many students, clients, and workshop participants over many years. It always works. I am indebted to those nurses who taught me so much.

My attitude changed too. Soon after, when employees made that remark to me, I would sit up straight and say, "This is the best job in the whole hospital." Sometimes, it was a lie. I hope this book will help you say those words as truth.

Roey Kirk, M.S.M.

Section 1

Developing the Unit of Service and Identifying the Department's Standard

Introduction: Getting Started

Managerial competence is a necessity for every healthcare manager. Many of today's healthcare managers entered their clinical fields for altruistic reasons and found that their clinical achievements and competence led to managerial promotions; others have taken the business or management school route. The awesome reality of today's healthcare environment can be frightening and frustrating for both. Healthcare professionals providing patient care or some other service spend time with patients (or their customers), know them and their needs (be it patient care or equipment repair), and, therefore, are the persons most knowledgeable about the quality of services delivered by their department. Sometimes this knowledge, is in conflict with the responsibility of maintaining budget goals. In today's competitive and cost-contained healthcare environment managers must be able to manage both if they are to survive and prosper.

To achieve this objective, healthcare managers need to know, first, that quality can be managed and, second, how to do it. Questions about how the manager can measure quality, quantify quality, and ensure quality on a daily basis, to both patients and staff members, must be posed, probed, and answered. Although the questions seem vague and unanswerable, there are specific and simple methodologies that can lead to their answers. Once the quality issue is correctly resolved, the information can be used as the core of budget and productivity systems.

This workbook contains ideas, methodologies, and forms that can be copied and used. As you apply them to your own situation, let them be a catalyst for revising and developing your own new ideas. Success belongs to those who combine their experience, imagination, and innovative ideas and focus on their objectives.

Service Units

The service that a department provides is the foundation of all departmental activities, from program and budget planning to productivity monitoring and evaluation. The **unit of service** is the common denominator that enables identification and measurement of activities in terms of both quality and quantity. Inpatient nursing departments use the **patient day**, with hours per patient day as the time measure; however, for all other departments, including outpatient nursing services, the unit of service is a **modality**. The following chart has some typical hospital inpatient and outpatient examples.

Department	Service Units or Modalities	Time Measure*
Emergency	Total visits	Hours per visit
Physical therapy	Treatments	Hours per treatment
Food service	Patient and cafeteria meals Dietitian visits	Hours per meal Hours per visit
Labor and delivery	Births	Labor minutes per birth
Surgery	Major and minor operations	Hours per operation
Laboratory	Tests	CAP† units
Public relations	Campaigns, brochures, press releases, etc.	Hours per project
Housekeeping	Square footage	Weighted square footage
Nursing–inpatient	Patient day	Hours per patient day (HPPD)

* Hours refer to labor or manhours worked, on the average, to deliver a particular service. Example: If there were 1,000 visits that took 1 hour of labor time and 1,000 that took 30 minutes, then the average visit would take 45 minutes ([60 x 1,000] + [30 x 1,000] + 2,000 = 45).

† College of American Pathologists.

Assigning Time Values to Service Units

When activities of patient care or related services are evaluated to determine consumption of staff labor hours, the activities and times can be accumulated and averaged to identify the **standard** care hours required per unit of service, which, in this case, is the modality. There should be a *predetermined* decision or allocation of time available for each unit of service. Here are some examples:

0.4	Respiratory therapy hours per patient modality (treatment)
1.0	Nursing care hours per cardiac rehabilitation modality (visit, exercise session)
0.5	Engineering hours per service modality (equipment repair)
.7	Multidisciplinary hours per emergency visit (.3 nursing, .2 physician, .2 other)

In the past, before we had to manage constantly within cost constraints, the standard labor hours were determined by and based on what was desirable to give the patient or consumer of the service. Now the desire and, indeed, the justification may be present to provide that level of service, but funding is less available. Thus, future service standards may be based not on what is desired or needed, but rather on what is affordable within the given reimbursement limitation. Healthcare managers will be challenged to create an environment of productivity whereby the desirable level of quality can be maintained under the mandated constraints.

Managers develop standards in different ways. Regardless of method, standards must be credible and validated before being approved for use. Once a standard is validated and deemed reliable (even among different raters and over a period of time), it can be used as the focal point of all departmental financial and quality planning. Planning based on an unreliable standard is like building a house on an inadequate foundation. It is very important to know and to be able to validate (1) what you want to do for the patient or client (e.g., a task) at a predetermined, and mutually agreed on, level of quality; and (2) how long it should take for competent staff to complete the task at the target quality level. By doing this, managers can plan their departmental workloads for maximum quality and financial benefit rather than hold their breath hoping everything will be okay.

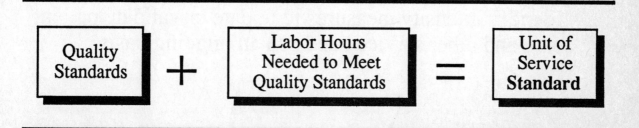

Supportive Information to Gather

Measuring labor hours consumed by patient care and other service tasks documents:

- Hours per modality (visit, procedure, test, service, etc.)

- Relative value units (of a predetermined number of minutes) per modality

Tracking the above data on logs or reports provides:

- Information about changing patterns (seasonal, market share) of resource labor hour consumption

- Retrospective data:
  - Modality intensity (acuity)
  - Modalities per discharged patient

Identifying volume and diagnostic distribution of current patients helps managers:

- Rank diagnosis categories to identify heavy users of the department's services by both volume and intensity

- Identify intensity measures to update or validate patient care and other service needs on an ongoing basis

Determining Standards

A department **standard** can be developed by (1) defining the measurable levels of quality that are routinely accomplished during the provision of a service; and (2) determining the length of time it takes to provide that service at the desired and previously agreed upon level of quality. There are several methods for determining standards for both modalities (procedures, tests, visits, chart transcription, services to other departments, etc.) and inpatient days. Some of these methods, along with their potential advantages and disadvantages, are listed below.

Estimating	The "best guess" approach. This method is low in cost, fast, and initially well accepted but is easily biased and doesn't always relate to current internal and external conditions.
Historical Averaging	This is the easiest and least expensive method. However, it is not necessarily precise; and with its use, existing deficiencies or inefficiencies tend to be perpetuated. Example: Stat Lab personnel worked 30,000 hours last year completing 90,000 modalities. **30,000 ÷ 90,000 = .33** care hours (20 minutes) per modality.
Logging	An excellent, low-cost method in which staff members are trained to log the activities and tasks they perform and the length of time it takes to complete them according to the predetermined performance standard. Logging can be used to identify and develop time values needed for patient classification system categories (initially and ongoing). Logs, such as **Activity Time Log**, Form 1.1, can be used to determine total time involvement by (1) modality, (2) classification category, or (3) standards of care.
Work Sampling	With this method, experts make random, instantaneous observations and, using statistical techniques, measure the relative time spent on various work elements. The expert is usually an outside source, such as a consultant, management engineer, or industrial engineer.
Predetermined Standards	With this method, industry-accepted standards and time studies, published as a service for information and implementation, are used. They are credible in that they have been scrutinized by professional leadership or have resulted from a research and development grant; but they might not be accurate in all cases. Individual institutions must analyze and assess applicability and acceptability of these standards.
Time & Motion Studies	This "clipboard" and "stopwatch" approach is task oriented. Each task is divided into motions that can be standardized, measured, and timed.

Logging and Documenting Activities

It is important to spend time determining accurate time values because they reflect our commitment of quality to a patient service. For most healthcare departmental budgets, a majority of the expense comes from personnel salaries. That expense relates directly to the labor time it takes to get the work accomplished. Thus, **validated time standards** for labor expenditure *per modality* can become (1) baseline data for the department's budget and productivity system and (2) a statement of commitment to a desired and predetermined level of quality care.

Activity Time Log, Form 1.1, is an excellent and inexpensive tool that can be used to determine department-specific standards for any task, from patient care activities to personnel office functions. Although a computerized or consultant-driven system may seem utopian and less stressful to staff members, both cost and quality benefits are realized when the department's staff members are involved in developing their own standards.

The logging method is simple and affordable. Staff members note on a log sheet, such as Form 1.1, the length of time it takes to complete a designated activity. Staff can keep logs on all their activities, or they can all work on one, an activity of the day, for example. The length of time an activity is studied depends on how quickly trends are identified and consensus is reached. Once a trend is identified (with supportive data), you can move on to the next activity. Later, if the activity changes or if the time no longer fits, the individual activity can be logged again for a "zoom in" look at how the staff's time is being spent. Some pros and cons on the logging technique for determining the department standard are outlined below.

Using Logging to Determine the Department Standard

- Provides a log sheet of work performed
- Records volume of work completed
- Displays activities and time values

PRO: Requires minimal training
Accounts for all time
Provides ongoing control
Applies to nonroutine duties
Is most readily accepted by staff
Logs individual productivity

CON: Disrupts employees
Is time consuming
Is inconsistent in terminology
Records exaggerations and errors

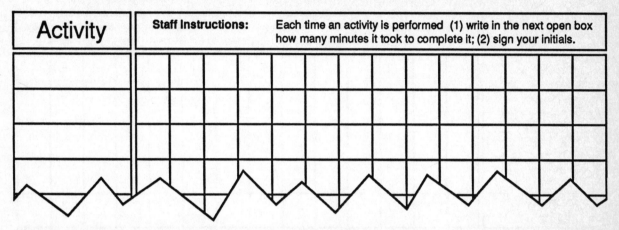

Activity Time Log
Assigning Time Values to Patient Care Activities

Activity	Staff Instructions:	Each time an activity is performed (1) write in the next open box how many minutes it took to complete it; (2) sign your initials.

Using this format to identify and validate time values can be economical, accurate, and informative. It can involve the staff, relying on their expertise (1) to sort through activities that are done simultaneously or in combination, (2) to note how long it takes to do an activity, and (3) to agree on a target for how long it *should* take to accomplish activities.

Benefits:

• *Average, or "most frequently used," times can be assigned to activities.*

• *Activities and their times accumulate in classification categories so that time values can be totaled and assigned to the category overall.*

• *Staff members who document fast times and demonstrate high-quality work can be tapped as resources to write those procedures and orient new staff.*

• *Staff members with slow times can be assisted in streamlining their work patterns.*

• *Staff members can document all their activities for a given period, or the unit can work collectively on an "activity of the day."*

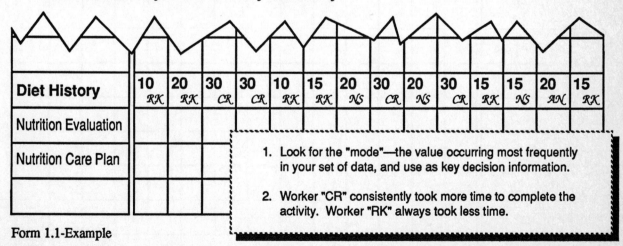

Diet History	10 RK	20 RK	30 CR	30 CR	10 RK	15 RK	20 NS	30 CR	20 NS	30 CR	15 RK	15 NS	20 AN	15 RK
Nutrition Evaluation														
Nutrition Care Plan														

1. Look for the "mode"—the value occurring most frequently in your set of data, and use as key decision information.

2. Worker "CR" consistently took more time to complete the activity. Worker "RK" always took less time.

Form 1.1-Example

Activity Time Log
Assigning Time Values to Patient Care Activities

Activity	Staff Instructions:																

Each time an activity is performed (1) write in the next open box how many minutes it took to complete it, (2) sign your initials.

For many departments logging and assigning time values to patient care activities is approached by using outside experts to do work sampling or time and motion studies. Usually, they do an excellent job of observing and identifying how long it actually takes to accomplish an activity. However, the staff member(s) being observed may be inefficient, or worse, may be performing an activity incorrectly. In that case, of what value would an average or accurate assessment of personnel time expenditure be? Furthermore, due to advancing technology and the constant change in supplies, methods, patients, and so forth, times that are appropriate today may become obsolete or outdated, even before the report is filed.

The best bonus of logging has to do with the expertise of the staff members and their ability to identify how long it takes to do the right things in the most efficient and effective way, which has a tremendous impact on quality. During the process of logging time values, if managers are wise, there is a real opportunity to look at activities in terms of patient care outcomes/results and performance standards, in relation to overall resource consumption. Involving staff experts in timing activities allows them to do a quick cost to benefit evaluation of each activity's worth.

Skeptical readers may be saying, "My staff will pad the time values." Rare though it may be, it probably will happen. In the end, however, there are only so many available/affordable hours. If staff are aware of constraints, they can use their expertise to identify ways to do the things they want to do, in the most efficient way, to stay within those constraints. Other skeptics may say their staff doesn't care; and, when it comes to productivity, they are probably right. When it comes to quality, however, staff members do care; it's why they are doing what they're doing. In addition, while they may not like planning this way, they'll surely prefer it over trying to do 10 hours of work in an 8-hour day. Employees already know that there is only so much money to spend, so it makes good sense to capitalize on their expertise and instincts about quality and use that information to maximize quality within existing productivity constraints.

Picture this utopian, but achievable, scenario. The manager of a radiology department talks with his/her staff about logging the length of time it takes to do various routine x-rays in the department. They decide to look at 10 specific x-rays that, in total, represent 90 percent of the department's total volume. They agree to begin the next day with logging only chest x-rays. The procedure (listed in the dusty black procedure manual on the shelf) is reviewed so that everyone will be using the same approach (at least at the start). At the end of the day, the staff take10 minutes (1) to review how long it took personnel to complete the task, (2) to identify if there is a consensus on how long the task *should* take, and (3) to reach a consensus on what the procedure should be and how long it should take to complete.

Once the care providers come to agreement, the time-valuing process for that activity is over. Time values will be looked at again after the budgeting process, if the hours required are more than what can be afforded. But, for now, efforts should be directed toward what we want to give to patients, the quality commitment. Who knows? Maybe it will end up being affordable.

At the end of a day when several clinical or technical specialists have been focusing their expert knowledge and experience on one activity, they are usually able to agree on:

- *what they should be doing for the patient;*
- *what the patient care outcomes should be; and*
- *how long the activity should take in terms of their time.*

Sometimes staff members do not reach a consensus, and there are discrepancies. For example, some may use different procedures, rather than the dusty, perhaps outdated, one from the book. Usually there are some staff memberss who are more efficient than others. Most have a preconceived notion of how long a procedure should take and fulfill that expectation, be it efficiently or inefficiently. The reasons can be endless, but one thing is always the same: At the end of a day, when staff members have been focusing their expert knowledge and experience on one activity, they are usually able to agree on what they should be doing for the patient, what the quality outcomes should be, and how long the activity should take in terms of their time. The answers may be a result of consensus, averaging, or adoption of one individual's efficient, and qualitative, way of doing things.[1]

Involving your own clinical experts in the initial logging and acuity development process creates a setting where staff members can contribute to defining standards of care and make their own contribution to outcome achievement. It also enables them to do their own, ongoing interrater reliability testing by comparing time results and patient care quality outcomes. Validity testing of time values will also be ongoing because each time staff members perform a modality, they can compare their knowledge of how long it *should* take with how long it *actually* takes. Then the factors that made the difference can be noted. The difference may be due to their own productivity level, a new or infrequently used procedure, a difficult patient, or a breakdown of a piece of equipment. Whatever the reason, their knowledge of the interference, combined with their expertise, is the best route to resolution.

---

[1] When this is the case, you should use efficient, expert staff members as resources to author the procedure and to train others and new employees. This reinforces to everyone that this is the way (i.e., the most efficient, effective way) we do this modality in our department.

Benefits of an Accurately Defined Service Unit

• *QUALITY* is protected by a predetermined, prioritized level of patient care or service performance by unit. Each unit has:

   - Verifiable standards of care or service as quality targets.

   - Measurable targets identifying the amount of time it takes to meet the standards.

   - A role in the total patient care plan; i.e., a group of timed activities that, when totaled, identify the patient's overall labor hour requirement for his or her total stay.

• *PRODUCTIVITY* methods can build on service units, which:

   - Define patient care and related service activities
      • At a prestated level of quality.
      • In terms of time, providing measurable targets for
         - planning future needs.
         - monitoring and evaluating productivity.

   - Help separate activities and rank them in order of priority.
      • Do we really need the service or activity?
      • Do we still want to provide it?

   - Break out the cost-benefit equation:
      • Cost–of professionally skilled labor.
      • Benefit–of quality patient care and related services.

Section 2

Using Patient Care & Service Standards for Budget Planning

Ensuring a Preselected Level of Quality

Quality–in a healthcare organization, this is an issue that is on everyone's mind: the patient, the care givers, employees providing ancillary or support services, management, physicians. Everyone wants it but they don't always agree on what it is and how to get it. It's not that we disagree; we just don't talk about it and, therefore, don't reach consensus regarding (1) what quality is, (2) how to achieve it, and (3) how to validate that it has been achieved. There is pressure on all of us, from regulatory agencies, accreditation bodies, and the marketplace to ensure a desired and prestated level of quality. This section will describe methods for managing the delivery of quality on a day-to-day basis.

The best way to ensure a desired level of quality for every patient on every day of his or her stay is to provide that quality on a unit-of-service basis, with a standard amount of patient care or service hours provided per modality. In the last section we talked about service units and how to identify the amount of labor hours consumed by different modalities in a department. In this section, we'll focus on applying those standard times, or hours per modality (HPM) to document staffing requirements and develop the personnel budget. We'll be building a classification system that will help us make quality- and productivity-based daily staffing decisions.

In this section, we'll assume that if standard time values have been set, they have been (1) validated (substantiated and verified for the amount of time they take) and (2) interrater reliability tested (two different, but equally skilled, staff members completing the task in the same amount of time and providing the same level of quality). These are important activities because we will be using standard time values throughout this text as baseline information for a variety of management systems. If we want the systems to hold up under pressure, we have to build a sound foundation. If you have not yet accomplished these activities, use the information below to guide your pursuit of this information.

Validity and Interrater Reliability Testing

Is the time standard valid?	Are all appropriate actions related to the modality included in the standard time?
	Have you received feedback or documentation from staff members indicating their consistent ability to complete the activity within the standard time?
Has the standard been tested for inter-rater reliability?	Are all staff members using the same processes, meeting the departmental standard of care for the modality, and taking the same amount of time to complete the task(s)?

There are a number of ways to identify the hours of staff member time consumed by patient care or services. For each organization and department, the best way must be decided given the individual situation. In one situation, department consensus will be sufficient; in another, management engineers will be called in to validate and test for reliability.[2] It is important for managers to do whatever is needed to ensure credibility and commitment to their standard time values. This is your business; and to manage it (as opposed to being an out-of-control victim of it), you must be able to define your product or service in terms of quality, productivity, and cost. In all cases, the standard time values must be credible, reliable, and approved for budgetary purposes. Even computerized calculations and standards developed by external consultants should be logged and audited periodically, as priorities of care and procedural practices of delivering services are continually affected by our dynamic and ever-changing healthcare environment.

---

[2] Validity and reliability testing can be done internally or externally (with the help of outside experts). In particular, if you (or your superiors) aren't comfortable with the time values you've come up with internally, spend the money to bring in experts. Just make sure there is a methodology that you can use for ongoing validity and reliability testing. Time values can potentially change with every new piece of equipment, method, or system.

Applications of Standard Time Values

Once established, standard time values for each modality or activity in the department can be accumulated over a period of time and used to identify the average patient care, or service, **hours per modality (HPM)**. *Standard HPM can be used as:*

- *The budget target per unit of service to ensure budgeted positions to meet the average volume and acuity needs;*

- *Productivity monitors: feedforward, concurrent, and retrospective;*

- *A baseline information that will guide managers in:*
  - *(1) hiring the right amount of staff for the right shift*
  - *(2) prescheduling staff according to accumulated classification data: average volume and average acuity*
  - *(3) making daily reallocation decisions based on actual classified acuity and volume;*

- *The determining factor in calculating the real cost of patient care or related services, pricing, and price control.*

Using Standard Time Values to Calculate Your Department's Hours per Modality (HPM)

Once time values for an individual modality have been validated and their inter-rater reliability has been established, they can be used by managers as a tool for ensuring the designated level of quality and productivity per modality. The first step in planning for this goal is to look at past trends over a period of time. The examples shown below and on the following pages are not for any specific length of time. Managers must assess strategic factors in their own department and then decide the length of time to study. Generally, looking at the last year will give a good overview; but if the trend has changed drastically in the last six months and is not expected to change back, only the last six months should be assessed.

Form 2.1, **Calculating Standards**, is designed to collect and classify volume and acuity information and can be used several ways. The example below is for a department that offers six different patient care services. The first column lists the six modalities (a generic term), however, in your own department you would simply list tests, procedures, or services that your department provides to patients or to another department in the organization. The second column shows the total number of times each modality was completed during the period being studied. The third column has predetermined standard time values for each modality. Calculations are made to establish the total staff hours required during the period.

Notice the difference between this example and the one on the opposite page. Same number of modalities, same time values, but a different distribution of services that were actually provided ultimately makes a big difference in the average required labor hours per modality. It would be impossible, given the same amount of

Calculating Standards
Using Retrospective Classification Data

Specific Department Modalities	Modalities Completed & Charged		Required Hours per Modality*		Staffing Hours Required
Modality # 1	0	X	.5	=	0
Modality # 2	0	X	.7	=	0
Modality # 3	0	X	1.0	=	0
Modality # 4	0	X	1.3	=	0
Modality # 5	2,000	X	1.5	=	3,000
Modality # 6	4,000	X	2.0	=	8,000
Totals	6,000				11,000

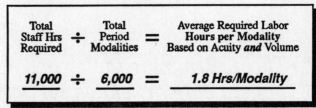

Total Staff Hrs Required	÷	Total Period Modalities	=	Average Required Labor Hours per Modality Based on Acuity *and* Volume
11,000	÷	6,000	=	1.8 Hrs/Modality

Form 2.1-Example A

* Hours exclude fixed (manager, clerks) and nonproductive hours paid for sick, vacation, holiday, etc. Classified hours address only direct, "hands-on" care.

Calculating Standards
Using Retrospective Classification Data

Specific Department Modalities	Modalities Completed & Charged		Required Hours per Modality*		Staffing Hours Required
Modality # 1	1,000	X	.5	=	500
Modality # 2	1,000	X	.7	=	700
Modality # 3	1,000	X	1.0	=	1,000
Modality # 4	1,000	X	1.3	=	1,300
Modality # 5	1,000	X	1.5	=	1,500
Modality # 6	1,000	X	2.0	=	2,000
Totals	**6,000**				**7,000**

Total Staff Hrs Required	÷	Total Period Modalities	=	Average Required Labor **Hours per Modality** Based on Acuity *and* Volume
7,000	÷	**6,000**	=	**1.2 Hrs/Modality**

Form 2.1-Example B

* Hours exclude fixed (manager, clerks) and nonproductive hours paid for sick, vacation, holiday, etc. Classified hours address only direct, "hands-on" care.

staff, to deliver the same level of quality in both instances, because the acuity (intensity of labor required) is so much higher in the first example.

It is not important at this point to consider operational factors such as how many shifts a day or days per week service is offered by this department. Right now our focus is on pure patient care or services by period. We'll distribute workload by day and shift in a later section.

The two additional examples (on this and the next page) are calculated the same way; but, instead of listing services as separate modalities, they are listed by length of time for their provision. This is a good method to use in departments such as physical therapy,

Calculating Standards Using Retrospective Classification Data			
Specific Department Modalities	Modalities Completed & Charged	Required Hours per Modality*	Staffing Hours Required
Modality - 30 min	0	X .5	= 0
Modality - 45 min	0	X .75	= 0
Modality - 1 hr	0	X 1.0	= 0
Modality - 1.5 hr	0	X 1.5	= 0
Modality - 2 hrs	2,000	X 2.0	= 4,000
Modality - 3 hrs	4,000	X 3.0	= 12,000
Totals	6,000		16,000

Total Staff Hrs Required	÷	Total Period Modalities	=	Average Required Labor Hours per Modality Based on Acuity *and* Volume
16,000	÷	6,000	=	2.7 Hrs/Modality

Form 2.1-Example C

*Hours exclude fixed (manager, clerks) and nonproductive hours paid for sick, vacation, holiday, etc. Classified hours address only direct, "hands-on" care.

or home care, where a variety of activities are completed within a given period. In these cases it is easier to track volume and acuity by grouping a selection of activities, and it is particularly successful when you can follow through with a relative pricing schedule that will provide additional revenue on patients using a greater amount of labor time. A word of caution if you use this strategy: Collect data to validate actual occurrences for each modality. You don't want to anticipate that all 6,000 modalities will require 2 hours (12,000 total hours) and experience the pain (in terms of both financial planning and staff utilization) of actually needing only 0.5 hours (3,000 total hours), or vice versa.

The goal is to target
average volume *and* **average acuity**
so that you can budget resources (personnel)
needed to provide anticipated services.

Calculating Standards
Using Retrospective Classification Data

Specific Department Modalities	Modalities Completed & Charged		Required Hours per Modality*		Staffing Hours Required
Modality - 30 min	1,000	X	.5	=	500
Modality - 45 min	1,000	X	.75	=	750
Modality - 1 hr	1,000	X	1.0	=	1,000
Modality - 1.5 hr	1,000	X	1.5	=	1,500
Modality - 2 hrs	1,000	X	2.0	=	2,000
Modality - 3 hrs	1,000	X	3.0	=	3,000
Totals	**6,000**				**8,750**

Total Staff Hrs Required	÷	Total Period Modalities	=	Average Required Labor **Hours per Modality** Based on Acuity *and* Volume
8,750	÷	**6,000**	=	**1.5 Hrs/Modality**

Form 2.1-Example D

*Hours exclude fixed (manager, clerks) and nonproductive hours paid for sick, vacation, holiday, etc. Classified hours address only direct, "hands-on" care.

Calculating Standards
Using Retrospective Classification Data

Specific Department Modalities	Modalities Completed & Charged	Required Hours per Modality*	Staffing Hours Required
_____	_____	X _____	= _____
_____	_____	X _____	= _____
_____	_____	X _____	= _____
_____	_____	X _____	= _____
_____	_____	X _____	= _____
_____	_____	X _____	= _____

Totals

Total Staff Hrs Required	÷	Total Period Modalities	=	Average Required Labor **Hours per Modality** Based on Acuity *and* Volume
_____	÷	_____	=	_____

* Hours exclude fixed (manager, clerks) and nonproductive hours paid for sick, vacation, holiday, etc. Classified hours address only direct, "hands-on" care.

Calculating Standards: Tip List

- Required hours per modality (HPM) can be derived from (1) one of the methods described in Section 1, (see Determining Standards); (2) a consultant's analysis; or (3) a professional association's assessment.

- If the people doing the work feel their department's time standards are inaccurate, do some more time studies and, if needed, problem solve!

- The **Calculating Standards** form can be used for any period, of any length—from one day to years—as the calculations are based on individual modalities and the corresponding required manhours.

- Modalities can be extracted from department logs or the business office records (charges are tracked). Occasionally, look at both to double-check count reliability.

Average Volume & Average Acuity - Why Are They Important?

Even when you've collected data with a vengeance, you may not be on target. Why? Because (at least as of this writing) no one has invented a crystal ball that really works. Planners and financial wizards have used many amazing and sophisticated techniques (I know one who keeps a Ouija Board™ under his desk) to predict what will happen in the future, but we never know for sure until that time arrives. The best we can do is (1) look at historical data—what happened last year or last period, (2) combine that information with our knowledge of what's happening in the marketplace and government, and to our patients, their families, our physicians, third party payers, and so forth; and, then, (3) plan for average volume and average acuity. If we plan for the average volume and average acuity, we'll be in the best position to react to actual volume and actual acuity on a daily basis.

Department and unit managers are in an excellent position to provide useful planning information; but, unfortunately, they are not always asked to participate in the process. However, some wise senior managers are actively involving mid-level managers in important strategic and long-range planning decisions impacting, or impacted by, their department because they have lots of good information and a keen sense of intuition about their departmental and related activities.

With all the strategic planning factors considered, the calculations completed on the preceding pages become the department manager's most powerful planning and management information. The average required hours per modality (acuity) combined with the average number of daily modalities (volume) is the best indicator of staffing requirements we have available. We've used that information in this section for budget planning; and we'll use it in the following sections for budget calculation, staffing pattern development, position control, prescheduling staff, and developing flexible scheduling options for our staff members.

While it is safe to assume in advance that the average acuity and the average volume usually won't occur daily on an ongoing basis, we have no idea what will occur. Planning for the average allows us the maximum flexibility for each day, to increase or decrease prescheduled staff to accommodate actual volume and actual acuity requirements. We are simply using all the information available to us to prepare in advance for the unknown. Every manager who has ever prepared a schedule knows that if the prepared schedules are short a staff member on Tuesday, that Tuesday will be the day that high labor-intense modalities will be ordered in record volume. The reverse is also true, so the best preparation is to plan for the average.

What If the Calculated Standard Is Not Approved?

While this section has been devoted to documenting and verifying the average HPM, it has been done with the knowledge that this action may not be enough to change the circumstances of tight budgets, hard times, and tough competition. Managers with documentation for increased staff may have their request for additional staff turned down because the need is due to an increase in acuity (which is not usually compensated for by charges) as opposed to an increase in volume of modalities (which is naturally supported by additional revenue dollars). Managers may be able to document need, substantiate it with facts, and validate results, and still have problems getting their standard approved for further use as their budget target. Many budget committees have already responded with statements indicating that they are aware that the patients are sicker and require more time per modality; but the money is not available to pay for additional hours.

So, what can a manager do if the standard isn't approved? Two different approaches can be taken. First, if the department already charges for its services, it may be possible to increase care hours according to classified needs and then to plan the charge structure to accrue more revenue for higher acuity modalities. This would allow additional labor hours (personnel) to be purchased as needed. When this option is available, the manager can try to get the standard approved based on the potential of increased revenue, or at least on sufficient revenue to cover the proposed labor expenses.

Second, the manager can go back and reanalyze the classification information, taking out activities that can be accomplished by a family member or another department, or streamlining the work that is done by staff members. All activities should be looked at again and prioritized according to standards of care and patient care goals so that the lowest priority activities can be designated as a "when time permits" activity. Standard time values that continually document the need for more care hours than are available or approved will create frustration for the staff and eventually will be viewed as a meaningless exercise, rather than as one of the most powerful patient care and service management tools available.

The manager's challenge is (1) to identify patient care needs in terms of labor hours, (2) to budget for those hours so that staff will be available to provide that service at a predetermined standard of care, or (3) to reorganize departmental workload so that it is compatible with the approved budget target HPM so the predetermined standard of care can still be delivered...with less staff hours.

Standard time values that continually
document the need for more care hours
than are available or approved
will create frustration for the staff and eventually will be
viewed as a meaningless exercise,
rather than as one of the most powerful patient care
and service management tools available.

Section 3

Using Patient Care & Service Standards for Budget Calculation

The Budget Process

Many managers think, incorrectly, that the budget is an allowance. In reality it is an ongoing process of planning for (1) the immediate months to follow and (2) the upcoming fiscal year. The primary goal for a department is to deliver services to the patient, or a patient care department, at a predetermined and agreed on level of quality. That quality is defined by both the standards of care and the unit of service, which describes how much time it takes, in labor hours, to deliver that level of quality. Thus funding is needed to hire sufficient personnel to provide "x" labor hours per modality (HPM), but no more than "x". That's where it gets tricky.

The budget is a plan...not an allowance.

- *What are my goals for the next year?*
- *What resources (labor, supplies, equipment) will I need to achieve these goals?*
- *What will those resources cost?*

Sometimes goals and plans are approved, but dollars are not. If you are working with this kind of constraint, it's better to know it first so you can plan for maximizing quality within the constraint.

This philosophy is particularly true when it comes to patient care departments. Their most important goal is to provide a target level of care. Having those hours and dollars budgeted doesn't ensure quality, but it does ensure adequate dollars for hiring and providing appropriate staffing. Budgeting and staffing become easy tasks once the standard HPM are identified and approved. The process begins by planning for "x" HPM for every single modality expected in the new fiscal year and ends with building the rest of the budget around it. In theory, using the budgeted HPM as baseline information protects quality by ensuring those HPM are available.

Calculating FTE Required for a Desired Level of Quality

Once the unit of service is established and validated, it can be used as the focal point of all personnel budgetary planning. It may seem like "numbers" will be dictating the plans for patient care, but it must be remembered that they are based on standards of care that identify a preselected level of quality. In calculating a budget, our primary goal is to identify the personnel (i.e., full-time equivalents [FTEs]) we need to hire (1) to our standard of care and (2) to stay within our budget target.

Full-Time Equivalents (FTE)

A full-time equivalent (1.0 FTE) is a position for one full-time employee or two or more part-time employees. It is equal to 2080 hours annually (40 hours per week for 52 weeks). If that employee cuts his or her working hours to 24 hours a week (3 days), then another part-time employee can be hired to work the other 16 hours (2 days) each week. For budgetary purposes the FTE positions, not individual employees, are approved. The chart on the top of the opposite page shows different ways an FTE can be split. Note that 4 days in a 2-week pay period is the standard relief for a 7-day per week position. The 1.0 FTE works 5 days, and the 0.4 FTE allows coverage for the full-time person's 2 days off.

In the following pages the flexible (or variable, as it is sometimes called) budget process is followed from the initial step of determining direct care manhours through the final outcome of total FTEs for the new fiscal year. Flexible budgeting is an easy process to learn if taken one step at a time; thus, the process is described in several sections. Taken together, they comprise the body of Form

Full-Time & Part-Time FTEs			
During 2-Week Period		**Annual Hours**	**Percentage of 1.0 FTE**
Days Worked	**Hours Worked**		
10	80	2080	1.0
8	64	1664	.8
6	48	1248	.6
5	40	1040	.5
4	32	832	.4
2	16	416	.2

3.1, **Acuity- & Volume-based Staffing Budget**, shown at the end of the section. Demonstrated in the graphs below is the difference among three budget systems: (1) A *fixed* budget system, where staffing remains constant regardless of variations in census; (2) A completely *flexible* system, in which increases and decreases in staffing are based on volume; and (3) A *semiflexible* system (the most frequently used in healthcare), in which approximately 10 to 15 percent of staff are fixed (i.e., staff who do not increase and decrease according to volume, such as clinicians, clerks, managers) and the remaining staff are flexible and volume adjusted. The semiflexible system is the example used in the following sections.

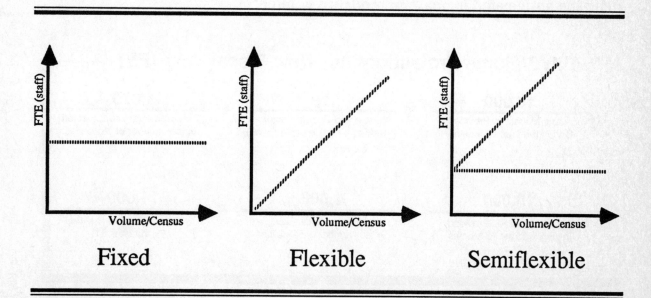

Volume

The first step in determining how many staff members you need for the new fiscal year (FY) is to predict, as closely as possible, what the volume or activity level will be in the new year. Is the service growing? shrinking? remaining constant? Historical data, market research, and communication with purchasers of health-care services (e.g., patients, physicians, third party payers, HMOs, PPOs) all provide information that will help support the guess. Every conceivable statistical, analytical, and computerized system has been used over the years to forecast volume (remember the financial wizard with the Ouija Board™ under the desk); but, normally, there is a variance between what is anticipated and what really happens. Using the average labor HPM (which describes the average patient care or service requirements) in combination with the anticipated volume will enable managers to react and adjust to changes in volume and acuity, on any shift, and successfully maintain the budget goal throughout the FY.

Volume: • *patient modalities (visits, tests, procedures, treatments, etc.) accrued year-to-date, or*
• *a projection of future demand*

The volume in the example below is forecasted to grow 10 percent annually in the next FY. Therefore, a 10-percent growth factor is used to mathematically accumulate the anticipated increase in modality volume.

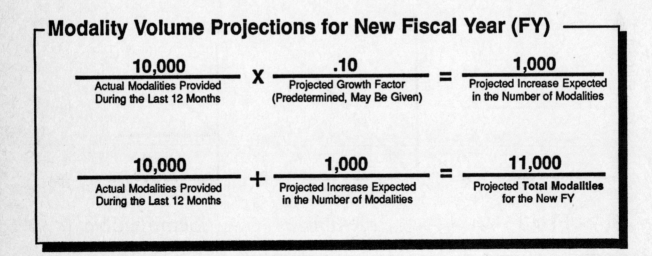

Modality Volume Projections for New Fiscal Year (FY)

10,000		.10		1,000
Actual Modalities Provided During the Last 12 Months	X	Projected Growth Factor (Predetermined, May Be Given)	=	Projected Increase Expected in the Number of Modalities

10,000		1,000		11,000
Actual Modalities Provided During the Last 12 Months	+	Projected Increase Expected in the Number of Modalities	=	Projected Total Modalities for the New FY

Flexible (Direct) FTE

Once the unit standard is validated it can be used in the volume-based approach to build a flexible budget. The objective (step #1 below) is to provide 1.0 HPM (the unit standard) for each of the expected and projected modalities. The next step (#2 below) is to divide the large number of hours by the number of hours a full-time equivalent (hereafter, FTE) works annually (2080 hours) to ascertain how many full-time positions are needed to deliver the direct care or service.

Flexible (direct) FTEs refer only to FTEs devoted to hands-on care of patients. In the illustration of the semiflexible budget (page 27), the diagonal line represents the action of volume-based adjustments that increase and decrease staff to match increases and decreases in volume. In step #2 of the example, 5.3 FTEs need to be hired just to guarantee every patient 1.0 hours of direct care for each modality, on the average. If the volume doubled to 22,000 projected modalities, the number of direct FTEs would also double because the goal remains the same—providing an average of 1.0 hours of care for every modality or service that is delivered.

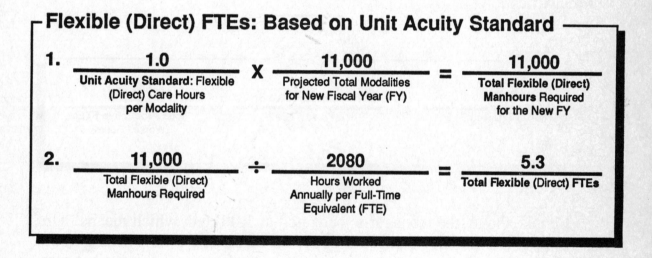

Flexible (Direct) FTEs: Based on Unit Acuity Standard

1. $\dfrac{1.0}{\text{Unit Acuity Standard: Flexible (Direct) Care Hours per Modality}} \times \dfrac{11{,}000}{\text{Projected Total Modalities for New Fiscal Year (FY)}} = \dfrac{11{,}000}{\text{Total Flexible (Direct) Manhours Required for the New FY}}$

2. $\dfrac{11{,}000}{\text{Total Flexible (Direct) Manhours Required}} \div \dfrac{2080}{\text{Hours Worked Annually per Full-Time Equivalent (FTE)}} = \dfrac{5.3}{\text{Total Flexible (Direct) FTEs}}$

Naturally, not every patient modality requires or receives exactly the same amount of direct care on a daily basis. Factors such as patient acuity, physician orders, and patient/family expectations and personalities play a part in how much time a staff member spends delivering a particular modality. These factors cannot be ignored and, in fact, should be considered and included in the logging and planning activities, which were completed in the first two sections of this book. Unfortunately, it is not until we get to the stage where we are looking at the personnel budget that we see the impact of not having enough, or the right kind of, data to document our patient care needs.

Fixed FTE

All labor hours are not volume related. Indirect care, such as work done by clerks, managers, or clinicians, for example, is not directly affected by the volume or acuity level; their workload may continue to increase even when the volume of ordered modalities is on the decline. The work of the manager, for example, can increase when the volume declines if staff members need to be reallocated or called off. In addition, for clinicians, some of the best opportunities for inservice education occur at these times. Over the long run, however, their work should decline proportionately with the volume of patient days, even though it is not directly related to the unit of service (the modality) and it is not flexible.

Careful planning is needed for allocating fixed FTE hours because fixed costs can be very expensive, particularly if the census declines and the workload of the fixed FTE increases. As is shown below (step #3), the 3.0 total fixed FTEs are simply added to the total flexible (direct) FTEs with no specific relationship to the number of those FTEs or the projected volume (although 10 to 15 percent is usually acceptable). Because fixed FTEs are not volume related, they require significant justification.

Fixed FTEs

3. $\dfrac{5.3}{\text{Total Flexible (Direct) FTEs}}$ **+** $\dfrac{3.0 \text{ (1.0 Manager, 2.0 Clerks)}}{\text{Total Fixed FTEs}}$ **=** $\dfrac{8.3}{\substack{\text{Total Productive FTEs}\\ \text{(Worked Hours)}}}$

In the example above, the manager is budgeted at 1.0 fixed, which means there are sufficient hours for the manager to spend all of the full-time working hours (40 hours a week) on management activities without affecting direct patient care. Other managers are not so lucky; and, in fact, when they work this step-by-step series backward using their own department, they discover that some or all of their hours are flexible, not fixed! When this is the case, the manager is tied to direct patient care, or if the manager does break away to do indirect work, the remaining hours for direct care or providing a service are reduced and the preplanned 1.0 hours of care are not delivered in total.

Managers should assess how much management work needs to be done and budget those hours as fixed (even if it's 1 day a week [.2 FTE]). Then they can take on additional responsibilities and be accountable for results.

Nonproductive FTE

The last group of hours to consider is nonproductive FTEs, the FTEs required for the sole purpose of covering the direct care FTEs when they are using paid benefit time (i.e., being paid, but not working). Paid time off for vacation, holiday, jury duty, death leave, sickness, and so forth, is a norm for full-time and, in many cases, part-time staff. Employees may be off with full pay for up to 6 weeks annually. If the time is approved without considering coverage for those absent employees, the HPM and standards of care will be impacted directly and dramatically. Thus, it is only sensible to plan, look ahead, identify the average benefit hours scheduled to be paid to department staff members, and calculate how many hours they'll be away and require coverage. Sometimes managers don't plan coverage, hoping that the census or acuity will be lower than normal, but that is a risk that often has to be covered with overtime pay.

Each staff member (step #4 below), on the average, earns and takes 15, 8-hour per day vacation days; 8, 8-hour per day holiday days; and 48 hours (6, 8-hour per days) of sick time according to the prior year's averages. The total (232 hours for each of the 8.3 FTEs) adds up to enough hours (1926 annually) to hire the equivalent of almost a whole FTE just to cover the 8.3 FTEs when they are on paid leave from the institution.

Nonproductive FTEs

4. $\dfrac{8.3}{\text{Total Productive FTEs}}$ **X** $\dfrac{232 \text{ (15 V, 8 H, 6 S x 8 hours)}}{\substack{\text{Nonproductive Paid Hours for}\\\text{Hours Not Worked (per FTE)}}}$ **=** $\substack{1926 \div 2080 = .9 \\ \text{Hours Required to Cover} \\ \text{Nonproductive Paid Time}}$

Note: If fixed FTEs are not replaced when they use benefit time, exclude them from this calculation and use only flexible (direct) FTEs.

The resulting 0.9 nonproductive FTE in the calculation above might create the impression that a full-time employee should be hired to cover vacations, holidays, etc. Every effort should be made to resist that temptation because one individual will not be able to provide the needed flexibility for a variety of coverage requirements. It's preferable to use part-time and per diem staff (1) to increase the number of people available to cover when, and only when, they are needed, and (2) to provide maximum flexibility to the manager to be able to grant staff members their first choice when they put in a request for time off.

Total Adjusted FTE

The sum of (1) flexible (direct), (2) fixed, and (3) nonproductive FTEs is the *total adjusted FTEs*. It is referred to as "adjusted" because fixed and nonproductive hours were added to the direct hours to protect direct care hours and to enable 1.0 HPM actually to be provided to patients. The total adjusted FTE figure becomes the position control (that is, the total number of FTEs that can be hired) for the next FY. The position control remains constant for the remainder of that FY unless there is an approved adjustment by the budget committee or administration. In today's environment most of the approved adjustments are strictly for increases in modality volume that have already occurred. However, because this is a flexible budget, flexibility has been built in and adjustments can be made on a shift-by-shift basis if (1) the census is up or down or (2) the acuity is up or down. Staffing can be adjusted using the baseline information of 1.0 HPM, on the average, to every patient modality.

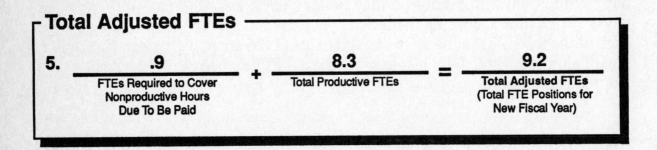

Total Adjusted FTEs

5. $\dfrac{.9}{\text{FTEs Required to Cover Nonproductive Hours Due To Be Paid}}$ $+$ $\dfrac{8.3}{\text{Total Productive FTEs}}$ $=$ $\dfrac{9.2}{\text{Total Adjusted FTEs (Total FTE Positions for New Fiscal Year)}}$

Adjusted Care Hours per Modality (HPM)

Adjusted care HPM are not included on the form but are interesting to know. They can be calculated by working backward from the *total adjusted FTEs*. In the example on the next page we are working backward from the 9.2 total adjusted FTEs result. The calculated *adjusted care HPM* indicates that to guarantee 1.0 HPM for direct patient care, the institution must pay for, or purchase, 1.7 hours of labor time. Direct care accounts for 1.0 hours of the labor expense, and the additional 0.7 hour covers overhead expenses of fixed FTE hours and paid benefit time. The number is extraordinarily high in this example because of low volume; also, the ratio of fixed and nonproductive FTE to flexible FTE is high, almost 1:1. We could reduce the ratio by either (1) reducing the fixed FTE or (2) increasing the volume, which would increase the direct/flexible FTE.

In some organizations, only the *adjusted FTEs* (also called "total paid FTE") are available to the manager. When this is the case, that information can be used to

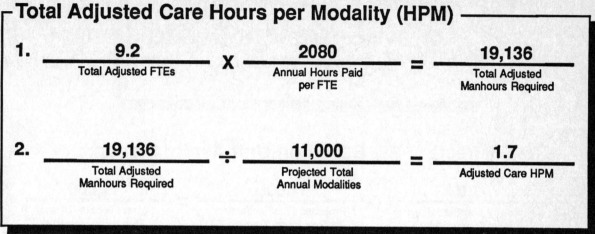

calculate adjusted HPM by taking the same steps we took in the example above. Even more important, they can use it to calculate their direct care hours per modality, which will let them know how many hours are available, or left, for direct care–the time staff members have left to spend delivering their service to patients. It is very important for the department manager to know the available direct care hours per modality. Without that information, quality standards and productivity targets cannot be set, much less worked toward, by department staff members. Even if the result is less than desired (e.g., only 0.8 hours are available, on the average, for modalities that the department manager knows require 1.0 hours), it is better to know that up front. If department managers know 1.0 HPM are required but the budget only allows for 0.8, they and their staff members can go back to their standard of care and make adjustments, streamline some of their procedures and eliminate others, or at least rank actions in order of priority. Another option is to use collected, and valid, data to fight (not to the death, however) to change it. Department managers may not like the answers when they calculate direct care HPM backward from the adjusted (total paid) FTE, but it is far better to know it so the situation can be addressed and, hopefully, resolved.

Acuity- & Volume-based Staffing Budget

The **Acuity- & Volume-based Staffing Budget**, Form 3.1, is an accumulation of all the calculations made throughout this section, with the exception of the adjusted care HPM (above). All department managers who have identified their department standard HPM can use this form to identify corresponding personnel requirements, an important step in justifying budgetary requirements. To maintain a desired level of quality there must be a direct relationship between the standard HPM and the total number of approved FTEs.

Acuity- & Volume-based Staffing Budget

Flexible (Direct) FTEs: Based on Unit Acuity Standard

1.
$$\frac{1.0}{\text{Unit Acuity Standard: Flexible (Direct) Care Hours per Modality}} \times \frac{11,000}{\text{Projected Total Modalities for New Fiscal Year (FY)}} = \frac{11,000}{\text{Total Flexible (Direct) Manhours Required for the New FY}}$$

2.
$$\frac{11,000}{\text{Total Flexible (Direct) Manhours Required}} \div \frac{2080}{\text{Hours Worked Annually per Full-Time Equivalent (FTE)}} = \frac{5.3}{\text{Total Flexible (Direct) FTEs}}$$

Fixed FTEs

3.
$$\frac{5.3}{\text{Total Flexible (Direct) FTEs}} + \frac{3.0 \text{ (1.0 Manager, 2.0 Clerks)}}{\text{Total Fixed FTEs}} = \frac{8.3}{\text{Total Productive FTEs (Worked Hours)}}$$

Nonproductive FTEs

4.
$$\frac{8.3}{\text{Total Productive FTEs}} \times \frac{232 \text{ (15 V, 8 H, 6 S x 8 hours)}}{\substack{\text{Nonproductive Paid Hours for} \\ \text{Hours Not Worked (per FTE)}}} = \frac{1926 \div 2080 = .9}{\substack{\text{Hours Required to Cover} \\ \text{Nonproductive Paid Time}}}$$

Total Adjusted FTEs

5.
$$\frac{.9}{\substack{\text{FTEs Required to Cover} \\ \text{Nonproductive Hours} \\ \text{Due To Be Paid}}} + \frac{8.3}{\text{Total Productive FTEs}} = \frac{9.2}{\substack{\text{Total Adjusted FTEs} \\ \text{(Total FTE Positions for} \\ \text{New Fiscal Year)}}}$$

Form 3.1-Example

Acuity- & Volume-based Staffing Budget

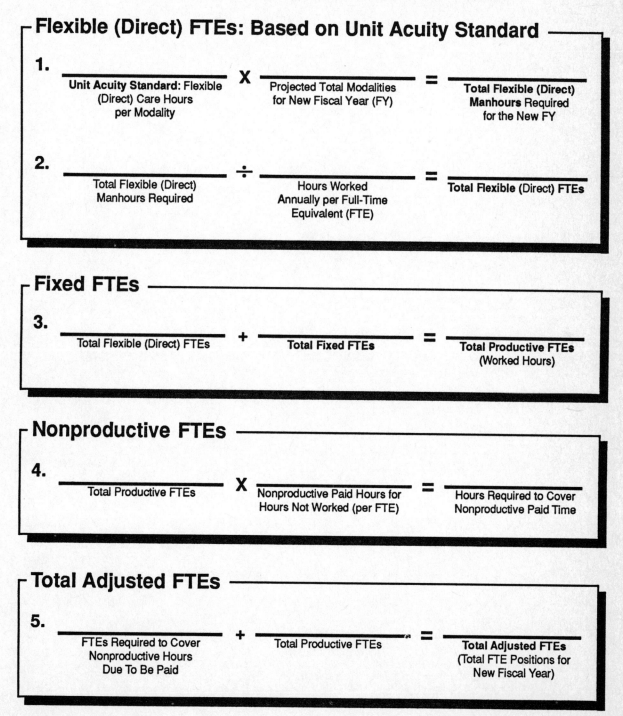

Flexible (Direct) FTEs: Based on Unit Acuity Standard

1.

| Unit Acuity Standard: Flexible (Direct) Care Hours per Modality | X | Projected Total Modalities for New Fiscal Year (FY) | = | Total Flexible (Direct) Manhours Required for the New FY |

2.

| Total Flexible (Direct) Manhours Required | ÷ | Hours Worked Annually per Full-Time Equivalent (FTE) | = | Total Flexible (Direct) FTEs |

Fixed FTEs

3.

| Total Flexible (Direct) FTEs | + | Total Fixed FTEs | = | Total Productive FTEs (Worked Hours) |

Nonproductive FTEs

4.

| Total Productive FTEs | X | Nonproductive Paid Hours for Hours Not Worked (per FTE) | = | Hours Required to Cover Nonproductive Paid Time |

Total Adjusted FTEs

5.

| FTEs Required to Cover Nonproductive Hours Due To Be Paid | + | Total Productive FTEs | = | Total Adjusted FTEs (Total FTE Positions for New Fiscal Year) |

Form 3.1

Section 4

Staffing Pattern Development

Using Standard Hours per Modality

Of the management functions, planning is the most important because all of the other management functions—organizing, staffing, leading, and controlling—build on planning premises and goals. Mutually agreed on goals are central to the entire management process.

- *Planning defines the goals.*
- *Institutions are organized and staffed to achieve goals.*
- *Leadership stimulates personnel to accomplish goals.*
- *Control compares actual outcomes with goal targets to evaluate results.*

Having the right amount of staff members on duty for an unknown volume of modalities with varying labor requirements is the result of careful planning, not happenstance. With such tight constraints on money, overstaffing in organizations delivering healthcare services can no longer be afforded. At some future time, staffing overages will ultimately result in either reduced profits or intentional understaffing if budget targets are to be met. In the past when hospitals operated under fixed budget systems, patients, rather than staff, fluctuated. On very busy days staff members worked like crazy, and on slower days (volume- or acuitywise) they recuperated. The patients receiving care on the busy days got far less, in terms of staff time and service, than the negotiated unit standard. On the other hand, patients needing care on the slow days sometimes received much more service than they were paying for, or expecting.

However, by determining a (1) unit standard of service and (2) corresponding hours per modality (HPM), there is the potential to build in a guaranteed level of quality. The combination of those two goals provides the initial planning steps to offering quality care to patients on a shift-by-shift, daily basis through the use of the unit **standard** HPM. However, there is a big jump from budget calculation to providing high quality patient care. The next step is developing the staffing pattern.

Once the standard is developed and approved, it can be used as the focal point in the development of a staffing pattern. A staffing pattern is simply the annual scheduling plan designed to accommodate the average census at the average acuity level. When staff members are routinely prescheduled according to such a plan, the manager is in the best possible position to reallocate them to meet unpredicted fluctuations in volume. Variations in modality acuity occur as well. Even when modalities are ordered as expected, a swing toward an older population, for example, may increase the amount of labor time expended per modality. Thus, you never know for sure. Managerial judgment, combined with planning for the average, creates more flexibility for reallocations when the actual day arrives. Managers need all the flexibility they can get because it seems on the days when staffing is short that the volume of modalities ordered always increases wildly, and our labor time is inhaled by each one.

Preparing Data for the Staffing Pattern

Continuing with the example from the last section, let's assume once again that the approved unit of service standard is 1.0 HPM. If 11,000 modalities were projected, then the **average daily volume** expected is 30 modalities (11,000 ÷ 365), on the average, if the department is open 7 days per week. The volume would be 42 daily (11,000 ÷ 260) if the department was open 5 days per week. The departmental goal in this case is to ensure 1.0 hours of care, on the average, to each of its modalities within a 24-hour period.

The underlying assumption is that if the average required hours are available, then the department is in the best position for the delivery of the desired level of quality. There are, of course, other factors to consider (i.e., Just because a staff member has enough time to do a procedure, it doesn't mean they will do it right.); but managing performance is a subject for another book. What we are working toward in this section is making sure that the approved hours (from the last section) are distributed in a deliberate pattern that will match the work flow and staffing requirements in the future. Because we don't know what will happen in the future, the best we can do is plan for what usually has happened in the past. By looking at past trends of average census and percentage of workload by shift we can predict with some accuracy and preschedule accordingly.

When the actual day arrives, volume is often higher or lower than expected and the average time required by modalities that were actually ordered will be higher or lower than the 1.0 HPM we budgeted. We anticipate that they'll probably be different, but we don't know in advance which way they'll go. So the tactic will be to plan for the average situation. We know from the last section that the average acuity is the unit standard, 1.0 HPM; and we've just calculated the average volume (on the previous page). Therefore, if an average of 30 modalities are anticipated, the manager should preschedule 30 labor hours daily (30 modalities x 1.0 HPM), or 3.75 staff working 8-hour shifts daily, as shown below. If an average of 42 modalities are expected, the manager should preschedule 42 labor hours daily (42 modalities x 1.0 HPM), or 5.3 staff working 8-hour shifts.

Operational 7 Days/Week	Operational 5 Days/Week	
30.0	42.0	Average daily modalities
x 1.0	x 1.0	Average direct HPM
30	*42*	***Hours required to staff the unit 24 hours per day***
÷ 8	÷ 8	Hours in a normal work day
3.75	*5.3*	***Target number of staff to be prescheduled daily***

For departments that are only open 5 days a week for one shift, the work is done. Five full-time employees and one part-time employee are hired, and that's what the daily staffing pattern will look like. However, for other departments that are operational 24 hours per day and/or 7 days per week, some decision must be made regarding the distribution of the workload. We can't just staff all of our employees on the day shift (7-3) and then put the patients or ordered services on automatic pilot for the 3-11 and 11-7 shifts (though it has been suggested). For each department a conscious decision must be made about workload distribution based on (1) the times patient care and service activities usually take place and (2) the availability of personnel resources. For example, if a department averages 30 modalities per day, with an average of 18 (60%) of those modalities being completed on the day shift, then 60% of the daily staff (.60 x 3.75 = 2.25) should be scheduled to work 7-3.

This is not entirely mathematics. The manager has to decide a couple of things. First, 2.25 daily staff can mean (1) two employees are scheduled and a part-time employee is scheduled 2 hours per day, or to come in early from the next shift; or (2) two employees are scheduled daily and 25% of the time a third person can be scheduled as needed. For example, if on Fridays the workload is notoriously heavy, then you might want to preschedule a third person.

Second, the manager may or may not be able to control the time the modalities are delivered, but he or she can control some of the indirect departmental workload. For example, if in the respiratory therapy department enough people for the 3-11 shift can't be hired and personnel on the 3-11 shift are currently responsible for cleaning the equipment, then equipment cleaning could be reallocated to the day shift, where hiring is less of a problem. Further, the manager may plan for equipment cleaning to be done between 3:00 P.M. and 5:00 P.M. so part-time staff available after school can be called in if needed. In a case like this, all workload should be analyzed to see if any part of the work can be redistributed to another shift without reducing the level of quality. It might mean one less rotation a month for employees who work the day shift.

On a daily basis, when there is an extra person scheduled on the 3-ll shift, and the 7-3 shift is short staffed, managers should be analyzing the workload to assess whether there is something that could be left for the afternoon or night shift. Unfortunately, for healthcare managers there are many variables over which we have little or no control. We must accept that and move our attention to the things we can control, and manipulate, in the interest of patient care and quality of our services.

Staffing Pattern Information

Illustration 4.1 (on the opposite page) shows an excerpt from the **Staffing Pattern,** Form 4.1. Here the department manager has decided (1) the department will be operational 7 days per week and (2) the workload will be distributed 60:40; i.e., 60 percent to the 7-3 shift, 40 percent to the 3-ll shift, with the department being closed during the night shift hours, 11:00 P.M. to 7:00 A.M. That means of 30 modalities 60 percent (18) will be delivered on the day shift and the remaining 40 percent (12), on the average, will be delivered on the evening shift. Because each modality takes 1.0 hours, on the average, and staff members work 8-hour shifts, we can calculate the number of staff needed for each shift using the formula on the top of the next page:

18 modalities x 1.0 HPM ÷ 8 hrs in shift = 2.25 staff on duty 7-3

12 modalities x 1.0 HPM ÷ 8 hrs in shift = 1.5 staff on duty 3-ll

Staffing Pattern

Department ___Cardio___

FTE: Flexible __5.5__

Staffing Pattern Planning Information

Shift	Percent of Modalities by Shift	Direct Hours per Modality	Expected Modalities	Daily Staff Scheduled*
7-3	60%	1.0	18	2.3
3-11	40%	1.0	12	1.5
11-7	0%	1.0	0	.0
3-Shift Total	100%	1.0	30	3.8*

Illustration 4.1

To deliver 1.0 HPM, on the average, managers need to preschedule 2.25 staff members on the 7-3 shift and 1.5 staff members on the 3-11 shift (Illustration 4.1, above). We are not distinguishing among different job categories that will contribute to the delivery of 1.0 HPM. This factor, however, should be considered, particularly because of differences of cost, and will be addressed when we discuss specific shift patterns later in the section.

In addition to splitting up the modalities by preselected percentages, the daily staff category, or actual employees assigned on-duty on a given day, should be split according to the same percentages. To staff to that pattern over a period of time, the total flexible (direct) FTEs (see Section 3) hired should be hired according to the same distribution. In the example on the previous page, and continuing below, 60% of the modalities occur on the 7-3 shift, (.60 x 30 = 18 modalities) so we should allocate 60% of our daily staff (.60 x 3.8 = 2.3 employees) and hire 60% of our flexible (direct) FTEs (.60 x 5.3 = 3.2 FTEs) for that shift.

Nonproductive (NP) FTEs can be handled at the discretion of the department manager. They can be allocated by modality percent (just as we did above), or they can be handled as fixed FTEs, where you would allocate them where you wanted. If the department manager, in this example, is already having trouble

ment *Cardiac Rehab*   **FY** *88* **HPM** *1.0*

exible *5.3* Fixed *3.0* NP *.9* Total *9.2*

tion

	Daily Staff Scheduled*	Flexible (Direct) FTEs	Non-productive FTEs	Fixed FTEs	Total FTEs
	2.3	3.2	.6	2.0	5.8
	1.5	2.1	.3	1.0	3.4
	.0	.0	.0	.0	.0
	3.8*	5.3	.9	3.0	9.2

Illustration 4.2

hiring for the 3-11 shift, he or she might consider putting all the nonproductive positions on the day shift so staff wouldn't have to work short on days if they were rotating to cover nights. Politically, if staff members are already angry about their rotations, the manager may not want to give the impression he or she has given up on hiring for the 3-ll shift. It's a judgment call and should be up to the manager who, in the end, has to live with the repercussions. As mentioned earlier, flexibility is the key to covering nonproductive hours. Hiring one full-time person to cover the benefit time of 5.3 other staff members will limit flexibility and the manager's ability to grant time off, as requested.

Most managers agree that benefit time is precious and should be given as requested whenever possible (as opposed to forcing someone to take time off at an undesirable time just because others are available to cover). Here are a few ways nonproductive hours can be handled to give maximum flexibility to both management and staff members. First, the nonproductive FTEs for several units can be combined to carve out a shared float pool of staff. Second, the nonproductive FTEs can be used to hire a group of per diem staff, rather than one individual to work 0.9, or 1872, hours per year. Third, if the unit already has a number of part-time staff members who are willing and interested in covering extra shifts, the 0.9 FTE position can be left vacant so that the funds are available to pay the already experienced part-time staff for the extra hours they work.

Fixed FTEs are the exception to the percentage rule. Fixed employees are assigned to the shift where they are needed to do their work. If 100 percent are needed on the 7-3 shift, that's where the corresponding FTE positions should be on the staffing pattern and where they will be assigned to work. Therefore, the assignment of 3.0 fixed FTEs (on the opposite) page is not related to the direct care distribution. There are 2.0 fixed FTEs (a manager and a unit clerk) on the 7-3 shift and 1.0 fixed FTEs (a unit clerk) on the 3-ll shift; and their assignments appear on the staffing pattern as such.

Performing all the calculations on the preceding pages may seem a long way around an activity that is already being accomplished, for the most part, through trial-and-error or sheer luck. However, the additional planning time at the beginning of the fiscal year will pay off in terms of fine tuning action plans directed at meeting budget and productivity targets. By starting out on the right track, it will be much easier to react to variations in volume and acuity without having to compromise quality, productivity, or budget targets.

Creating the Daily Staffing Pattern

If the work on the preceding pages has been completed properly, creating individual shift staffing patterns should be easy. Looking at just the 7-3 section of the staffing pattern, in Pattern 4.1 (right), and taking the information from Illustrations 4.1 and 4.2, we can build a pattern that will accommodate employees at a variety of skill or pay levels. The fixed positions are

7-3	Daily	Total
Flex:		
Flex:		
Flex:		
NP:		
NP:		
Fixed: **Manager**	**1.0**	**1.0**
Fixed: **Clerk**	**1.0**	**1.0**
Total 7-3 FTE		

Pattern 4.1

the easiest to place in the pattern because they are approved for 1.0 FTE each. That means there are enough hours and dollars for employees in those positions to work 5 days per week, but there's no coverage for their 2 days off each week (thus, 1.0 daily and 1.0 total). That would entail adding another 0.4 FTE for each of the fixed positions (see Section 3, *Fixed FTE*).

7-3	Daily	Total
Flex:		
Flex:		
Flex:		
NP: **RN**	**.0**	**.6**
NP:		
Fixed: **Manager**	**1.0**	**1.0**
Fixed: **Clerk**	**1.0**	**1.0**
Total 7-3 FTE		

Pattern 4.2

In Pattern 4.2 (left), the nonproductive FTEs are placed in the pattern. Again, this is fairly simple because the nonproductive FTEs only work when staff from the daily staffing pattern are using benefit time. Therefore, the 0.6 nonproductive FTE should not be counted in the daily column but should be shown in its entirety in the total column, because the hours are part of the total FTE. It is not crucial to break down nonproductive positions by skill level in the staffing pattern because they are replacement staff, but some managers prefer to be more specific. Pattern 4.2 also shows that all nonproductive FTEs on the 7-3 shift are budgeted as RN positions. Because this is a cardiac rehabilitation department and the staff comprises nurses, registered physical therapists (RPTs), and aides, the manager could have decided to cover 0.3 nonproductive FTE with an RN and the other 0.3 with an aide or an RPT. Again, this is up to the manager and depends on how specific he or she wants the pattern to be.

In the next step, flexible FTEs are placed in Pattern 4.3 (shown to the right). Using Illustration 4.1, there can be a total of 2.3 staff members scheduled on duty daily. Because they are on duty 7 days per week, each position requires 1.4 FTEs for 7-day coverage; and, thus, 3.2 flexible (direct) FTEs (2.3 x 1.4 = 3.2) have been budgeted so that the daily pattern can be achieved.

7-3		Daily	Total
Flex:	RN	1.0	1.4 ①
Flex:	RPT	1.0	1.4
Flex:	Aide	.3	.4
NP:	RN	.0	.6
NP:			
Fixed:	Manager	1.0	1.0
Fixed:	Clerk	1.0	1.0
Total 7-3 FTE		4.3 ②	5.8

Pattern 4.3

Note #1: For every FTE working 7 days per week, 1.0 covers the 5 on-duty days but another 0.4 is needed to cover the 2 days off.

Note #2: In the reality of a schedule, 4.3 FTEs daily means that there are four staff scheduled on duty every day, and for 3 days during the two-week pay period a fifth person could be added.

In the last example, the manager has the opportunity to fine tune and make minor adjustments to the pattern based on how well the pattern fits in with the reality of his or her individual staffing and hiring situation. For example, in Pattern 4.4 (on the next page), the manager has made the decision to change 0.1 of the "total" nonproductive RN FTE to RPT to be able to hire a 0.5 part-time RPT who will work three days one week and two days the next. The manager did this again to allocate 0.1 to the total RN to bring it up to 1.5. A small change, but a strategically significant move, because in some organizations a 0.5 part-time employee is entitled to benefits. Moving the 0.1 FTE to create a 0.5 position may attract new

7-3

		Daily	Total
Flex:	**RN**	**1.0**	**1.5**
Flex:	**RPT**	**1.0**	**1.5**
Flex:	**Aide**	**.3**	**.4**
NP:	**RN**	**.0**	**.4**
NP:			
Fixed:	**Manager**	**1.0**	**1.0**
Fixed:	**Clerk**	**1.0**	**1.0**
Total 7-3 FTE		**4.3**	**5.8**

Pattern 4.4

employees for both of these professions that are dealing with shortages. It's a little change, but one that may make a big difference when it comes to recruiting for these positions. Similarly, while some managers do not feel a 0.8 position is very attractive for hiring purposes, other managers really like and support the 32-hour work week as a norm for full-time staff (hired into a 0.8 position) because it allows the department 8 hours of straight pay (as opposed to overtime pay) to use during census increases.

Note that no changes were made to the daily column of the staffing pattern. Managers have ample opportunity, however, to adjust that when they get to the pre-scheduling process (Section 6) and on a daily basis as they reallocate staff according to actual need.

When the pattern is complete it will look like the **Staffing Pattern**, Form 4.1-Example (shown on the opposite page). This provides the manager with a sensible format to follow when completing time schedules throughout the fiscal year.

The blank forms following the example have been developed and provided in two different formats: (1) **Staffing Pattern**, Form 4.1, is the same as the example form and (2) **Staffing Pattern**, Form 4.2, is a modified version designed only for the final staffing pattern. Either one is acceptable.

Staffing Pattern

Department _Cardiac Rehab_ FY _88_ HPM _1.0_

FTE: Flexible _5.3_ Fixed _3.0_ NP _.9_ Total _9.2_

Staffing Pattern Planning Information

Shift	Percent of Modalities by Shift	Direct Hours per Modality	Expected Modalities	Daily Staff Scheduled*	Flexible (Direct) FTEs	Non-productive FTEs	Fixed FTEs	Total FTEs
7-3	60%	1.0	18	2.3	3.2	.6	2.0	5.8
3-11	40%	1.0	12	1.5	2.1	.3	1.0	3.4
11-7	0%	1.0	0	.0	.0	.0	.0	.0
3-Shift Total	100%	1.0	30	3.8*	5.3	.9	3.0	9.2

* Annual Modalities ÷ Work Days in Year (365, or 260 if closed 2 days per week) **x Standard ÷ 8 hours**

7-3

		Daily	Total
Flex:	RN	1.0	1.4
Flex:	RPT	1.0	1.4
Flex:	Aide	.3	.4
NP:	RN	.0	.6
NP:			
Fixed:	Manager	1.0	1.0
Fixed:	Clerk	1.0	1.0
Total 7-3 FTE		**4.3**	**5.8**

3-11

		Daily	Total
Flex:	RN	1.0	1.4
Flex:	RPT	.5	.7
Flex:			
NP:	RN	.0	.3
NP:			
Fixed:			
Fixed:	Clerk	1.0	1.0
Total 3-11 FTE		**2.5**	**3.4**[†]

11-7

		Daily	Total
Flex:			
Flex:			
Flex:			
NP:			
NP:			
Fixed:			
Fixed:			
Total 11-7 FTE			

[†] It is acceptable to make *minor* adjustments. Note changes from **information** calculation (Total FTEs column) above.

Form 4.1-Example

Staffing Pattern

Department_____ FY____ HPM____

FTE: Flexible_____ Fixed_____ NP_____ Total_____

Staffing Pattern Planning Information

Shift	Percent of Modalities by Shift	Direct Hours per Modality	Expected Modalities	Daily Staff Scheduled*	Flexible (Direct) FTEs	Non-productive FTEs	Fixed FTEs	Total FTEs
7-3								
3-11								
11-7								
3-Shift Total	100%							

* Annual Modalities ÷ Work Days in Year (365, or 260 if closed 2 days per week) **x Standard ÷ 8 hours**

7-3

	Daily	Total
Flex:		
Flex:		
Flex:		
NP:		
NP:		
Fixed:		
Fixed:		
Total 7-3 FTE		

3-11

	Daily	Total
Flex:		
Flex:		
Flex:		
NP:		
NP:		
Fixed:		
Fixed:		
Total 3-11 FTE †		

11-7

	Daily	Total
Flex:		
Flex:		
Flex:		
NP:		
NP:		
Fixed:		
Fixed:		
Total 11-7 FTE		

† It is acceptable to make *minor* adjustments. Note changes from **information** calculation (Total FTEs column) above.

Form 4.1

Staffing Pattern

Department_____

FY___ HPM____

FTE: Flexible _____
      Fixed _____
      NP _____
      Total _____

7-3

	Daily	Total
Flex:		
Flex:		
Flex:		
Flex:		
Flex:		
Flex:		
NP:		
NP:		
Fixed:		
Fixed:		
Fixed:		
Total 7-3 FTE		

3-11

	Daily	Total
Flex:		
Flex:		
Flex:		
Flex:		
Flex:		
Flex:		
NP:		
NP:		
Fixed:		
Fixed:		
Fixed:		
Total 3-11 FTE		

11-7

	Daily	Total
Flex:		
Flex:		
Flex:		
Flex:		
Flex:		
Flex:		
NP:		
NP:		
Fixed:		
Fixed:		
Fixed:		
Total 11-7 FTE		

Form 4.2

Section 5

Prospective Budget Control

Planning Ahead for "On Target" Performance

Budgetary requests for employees or FTEs are approved through the allocation and assignment of funding. The approval implies a serious responsibility for the healthcare manager to achieve his or her goals; i.e., (1) to ensure delivery of the target level of quality and (2) to achieve the target while spending no more than the approved amount of money. In a **fixed** budget system the annual salary budget remains constant even when there is an unexpected change in volume or acuity.

For example, if, for radiology department, the annual salary budget was approved for $400,000 for delivering 8,000 modalities (an average cost of $50 per modality) but, in actuality only 5,714 modalities were delivered, the average actual department cost per modality would be $70 ($400,000 ÷ 5,714 modalities), well over the targeted $50. On the other hand, if the actual volume was 10,000 modalities and the total salary costs remained the same, the average actual cost per modality to the department would be only $40.

In the long run, either case may seem to be acceptable as long as the total annual expense doesn't exceed $400,000. However, if we look only at dollars then there is no assurance

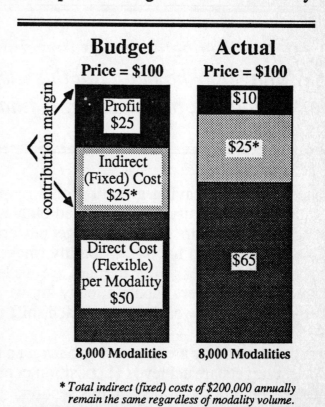

Budget Price = $100	Actual Price = $100
Profit $25	$10
Indirect (Fixed) Cost $25*	$25*
Direct Cost (Flexible) per Modality $50	$65
8,000 Modalities	8,000 Modalities

contribution margin

* *Total indirect (fixed) costs of $200,000 annually remain the same regardless of modality volume.*

indicates less than targeted spending for staffing and might be red-flagging a dangerous short-staffing situation. A fixed salary budget tends to lead to a fixed staffing pattern; i.e., 6 staff members are scheduled daily, every day. On the busy days staff members hussle; on the slow days they recuperate. However, if the intensity (or acuity) of the workload on day #1 was 50% heavier than on day #2, it would be impossible to deliver the same standard of care, at the same level of quality, on both days. The staff on day #2 would have to work harder and faster; yet, there would be no change in the price of the services between the two days.

In a **flexible** budget system, the **$50 per modality** (mentioned in the example on the previous page) represents a predetermined level of quality and time (and corresponding dollars) it takes to provide that standard of care. It becomes a **target** to work toward, instead of an annual budget allowance. If the annual projected modalities were 6,000 with a budget allocation for $300,000 ($50 per modality), and the actual census rose to 7,000 modalities, then the department manager could justifiably increase staffing and corresponding expense up to $350,000 ($50 target x 7,000 modalities). Looking at the total and/or salary costs per modality on a biweekly basis, along with the actual volume, will generally give a good indication of a manager's performance in controlling the budget and quality.

---

*Budgeted **hours** and **dollars per modality**:*
Managers who maintain this target create an environment
where quality, productivity, & financial standards can be met.

The purpose of having a section on **Prospective Budget Control** is to show managers how to use their approved budgets for planning and monitoring, prospectively, to ensure on-target budget performance; i.e., to manage it, rather than just to hope it will happen. Monthly financial and productivity reports that are published six weeks after the fact are useless except to reconfirm information healthcare managers should already know. It is far better to plan ahead, set up systems, and know each day and each shift that budget performance is on target.

There are two key areas within a manager's influence that impact whether or not budget targets are achieved (1) position control and (2) staff performance. We'll address both of these areas in this section.

≡ External Variables ══════════

Economic Variables:
Unstable economy
Forced competition
Cost-based to case-mix reimbursement
Cost accounting
Resources (3Ms: man/woman,
materials, machinery) availability

Political/Legal Variables:
Impact of partisan politics
Deregulation (or ultraregulation)
Prospective payment system
Malpractice

Technological Variables:
Cost
Availability
Design focus on reducing cost of care
Advantages of technology:
Monitoring capabilities
Reduction of working hours
Convenience
More accurate clinical information
Disadvantages of technology:
Expense
Increased manhours
Obsolescence
Quality-of-life issue

Ethical & Social Variables:
Quality-of-life issue
Personal value system conflicts
Health care access: Right vs. privilege
Politics of health care organizations
Hospital responsiveness to changing
demographics and social issues
Hospital role change: From controller
to coordinator

≡ Internal Variables ══════

Resources (the 3 Ms):
Allocation
Availability
Staff member demographic profiles
Staff mix

Infrastructure:
Organization's mission statement
Organizational structure
Organizational goals and objectives
Policies and procedures
Customs and practices

External and Internal Variables

Variability is a norm in healthcare. Unpredictable swings in volume or acuity can be a result of (1) **external variables**, such as economic stability, technological advances, social mores, ethical trends, or the political climate; and/or (2) **internal variables**, such as the infrastructure, availability of resources, or an organization's mission. Before embarking on position control and planning specific actions managers can take to control budgeted expenses, healthcare managers should be aware of the external and internal variables (listed above) and consider how they affect quality and cost efficiency in their own organization.

With so many different external variables affecting healthcare organizations, in general, and even more internal variables affecting patient care, services, and the internal management structure, the task of maintaining the budget can seem overwhelming at times. However, if managers can focus their attention on their own department quality and productivity targets and maintain them, on a shift-by-shift basis, both short- and long-range results can be predicted and achieved.

Position Control

Budget planning and calculation are done, in part, to help manage a budget after it is approved. With competition in the healthcare industry continuing to increase, more and more attention will be paid to a manager's ability to control the departmental budget and keep the budgeted labor hours per modality (HPM) in agreement with the predetermined target. When the final budget is approved for a particular number of FTEs (in the example used in Section 3, 9.2 Total FTEs were approved), those FTEs become the department **position control**, or the number of FTEs that can be on the payroll at any given time. This is an important number to remember!

The actual census will go up and down, as will the acuity, or intensity, of actual modalities; and the number of staff assigned should go up and down accordingly. However, *the position control remains rigidly constant throughout the fiscal year unless there is a mid-year, volume-based adjustment approved after several months of demonstrated volume increase.* Even after the approval, the increase should be conservative as volume seems to take a nose dive the day after additional staff members are hired to meet previously documented increases in volume.

> *One **key** factor in managing a personnel budget is resisting the temptation to overhire.*

One way to track positions, and the people who are hired into them, is to use a form like the **Position Control**, Form 5.1. It is shown on the following pages in two different ways: (1) Form 5.1 is a blank copy of the form suitable for copying and your own use and (2) Form 5.1-Example is filled in as it would be for any department. The corresponding footnotes are on the page opposite the example.

Position Control

Position Title	Hours	FTE	Name #1	Name #2	Name #3

7-3 Shift Total = ___ Flexible (Direct) + ___ Nonproductive + ___ Fixed = ___ FTEs

Position Title	Hours	FTE	Name #1	Name #2	Name #3

3-11 Shift Total = ___ Flexible (Direct) + ___ Nonproductive + ___ Fixed = ___ FTEs

Position Title	Hours	FTE	Name #1	Name #2	Name #3

11-7 Shift Total = ___ Flexible (Direct) + ___ Nonproductive + ___ Fixed = ___ FTEs

DEPARTMENT TOTAL FTEs = _____

Form 5.1

Position Control

Footnotes to circled numbers are on the opposite page

Position Title	Hours	FTE	Name #1	Name #2	Name #3
Respiratory Therapist - II	2080	1.0	J. Jones		
RT - II	2080	1.0	~~C. Hunt~~	J. Greenfield **❸**	
RT - II *(modified full time)* **❶**	1664	.8	J. Karaboyas		
RT - II *(nonproductive)*	416	.2	Y. Kieval *(PD)* **❹**		
RT - II *(nonproductive)*	416	.2	B. Drew *(PD)*		
RT - II *(nonproductive)* **❷**	416	.2	T. Kirk *(PD)*		
RT - II *(nonproductive)*	416	.2	L. Laher *(PD)*		
RT - II *(nonproductive)*	416	.2	M. David *(PD)*		
Respiratory Therapist - I	2080	1.0	F. Drury *(RT - II)* **❺**		
RT - I	832	.4	B. Blair *(.5)* **❻**		
RN Clinician	2080	1.0	D. Kranz		
Technician/Aide	2080	1.0	D. Russell		
Technician/Aide	2080	1.0	C. Todaro		
Secretary	2080	1.0	J. Hicks		
Manager	2080	1.0	B. Joyce		

7-3 Shift Total = 7.2 Flexible (Direct) + 1.0 Nonproductive + 2.0 Fixed = 10.2 FTEs

Position Title	Hours	FTE	Name #1	Name #2	Name #3
Respiratory Therapist - II	2080	1.0	M. Morrell		
RT - II	1040	.5	M. Fushmann		
RT - II	1040	.5	R. Johnston		
RT - II	1040	.5	E. McClure		
RT - II	626	.3	A. Lawrence		
Respiratory Therapist - I	2080	1.0	H. Hoesing		
RT - I	832	.4	L. Thompson		
RT - I *(nonproductive)*	1248	.6	*Do not fill* **❼**		
Technician/Aide	1040	.5	P. von Ellen		
Technician/Aide	1040	.5	P. von Ellen		
Technician/Aide	832	.4	V. Smith		
Secretary	2080	1.0	B. Meyerson		

3-11 Shift Total = 5.6 Flexible (Direct) + 0.6 Nonproductive + 1.0 Fixed = 7.2 FTEs

Position Title	Hours	FTE	Name #1	Name #2	Name #3
Respiratory Therapist - II	2080	1.0	K. George		
RT - II	832	.4	~~H. Townson~~	~~D. Michael~~ **❽**	
Respiratory Therapist - I	2080	1.0	J. Peterson		
RT - I	832	.4	S. Larken		
RT - I *(nonproductive)*	832	.4	*Do not fill*		
Technician/Aide	626	.3	*Do not fill*		

11-7 Shift Total = 3.1 Flexible (Direct) + 0.4 Nonproductive + .0 Fixed = 3.5 FTEs

❾ *DEPARTMENT TOTAL FTEs = 20.9*

Form 5.1-Example

Footnotes: Position Control (Form 5.1-Example)

The example on the opposite page shows how the **Position Control**, Form **5.1** can be used to help manage the hiring of personnel within approved budget constraints. The circled numbers correspond to the numbers below.

1. If there is a program for hiring **full-time staff for less than a 40-hour week** (a 32-hour week is used in this example), only the guaranteed hours should be reflected in the position control, because any additional hours would be a result of increased volume and corresponding revenue.

2. **Nonproductive** hours should be separated and identified on the Position Control form so they are not confused with direct care hours/FTE. Identifying them separately will also serve as a reminder to preschedule vacations evenly throughout the fiscal year.

3. When **positions turn over**, the name of the employee who left should be eliminated, and the new hire's name should be recorded.

4. **Per diem (PD) staff** are scheduled to work only when needed and can be called off at the last minute if census declines. They have few or no employee benefits and sometimes are employed by an outside agency.

5. This is an example of how to note an employee being hired into a position with a job description different than his or her own. In the example, an **RT-II was hired into an RT-I position**, and the overage will show up in dollars but not in hours. This would probably require administrative approval.

6. Occasionally staff are **hired to work more hours than available for the budgeted position**. In the example, a 0.5 part-time employee was hired into a 0.4 opening. It might have been done to help cover for a vacancy elsewhere in the budget; but, whatever the reason, it should be noted for future reference.

7. The decision was made to **use per diem staff to cover nonproductive** time off. One full-time person could not possibly cover benefit days or unexpected absences with as much flexibility and cost efficiency.

8. A blank space, or a name with a line through it, reflects a position that has been **vacated** by an employee termination **and not yet refilled**. This might be a result of either an inability to find an appropriate replacement or, possibly, a manager's reaction to a lower than budgeted (anticipated) census.

9. The sum of the 7-3, 3-ll, and 11-7 shifts' total FTEs.

Performance Appraisal Systems: Personnel's Role in Prospective Budget Control

Once position controls are in place, the healthcare manager's next challenge lies in recruiting, selecting, and hiring the best staff to meet the quality and budgetary goals. Traditional benefits of the performance appraisal process are fairly well known; however, this process is also very useful as a way (1) to prospectively manage the budget, by using job descriptions and evaluation criteria to negotiate several kinds of formal prehiring agreements; and (2) to facilitate initial and ongoing communication of job responsibilities and standards that are designed to provide prospective and ongoing budget control.

The duties, responsibilities, expectations of performance, and standards that will be used for evaluation allow prospective candidates to make an informed decision about their fit with the organization. Job descriptions and performance evaluations that are criteria based and developed according to standards of expected performance provide interviewing employees with a clear understanding of their duties, responsibilities, and evaluation criteria. This type of performance appraisal process has replaced the "trait" or "character" type of job description or evaluation. Each is described below.

Approaches to Describing Skills and Competencies

Trait	*Criteria Based*
Handles stress well	Maintains predetermined level of performance when under stress
Has telemetry experience	Is able to operate telemetry equipment unassisted and interpret results
Is certified in cardiopulmonary recuscitation and has code experience	Assesses and, when necessary, initiates approved procedures for patients in cardiopulmonary arrest

Job Standards Provide Prospective and Ongoing Budget Control

The overall budgetary savings result from carefully constructed job responsibilities and performance standards.[3] Employees who know what is expected of them, in terms of results, and who have a verifiable, measurable goal to work toward are more likely to be successful. Thus, if cost containment is an important institutional goal, then the employee's responsibility for cost containment should be so stated, along with performance standards that identify measurable results for future evaluation based on those indicators. The last job responsibility described on the next page is one example of a cost-containment performance standard.

The examples on the following page demonstrate that any job duty or responsibility can be accompanied by a verifiable way of measuring whether or not the employee has met the standard, exceeded the standard, or needs to continue to work toward meeting the performance standard.[4] At the worst, the employee knows exactly what to do to improve and at what point performance will be acceptable. At the best, every employee (1) knows exactly what is expected in terms of performance, (2) can self-evaluate throughout the year, and (3) can maintain his or her peak performance.

Prehiring Agreements

Prehiring agreements are negotiations that take place with potential employees before hiring. Usually, this process includes reviewing the job description, policies, departmental procedures, and benefits. However, when job expectations and expected results are also defined (in measurable, verifiable standards of performance) and communicated to an employee during the initial interview, the benefits of prehiring agreements increase in a number of ways:

1. When performance standards are defined and written, candidates can decide before accepting the position if they are able and willing to work toward the position's prestated goals.

2. When position issues and responsibilities are discussed before an employee is hired, the interviewer and candidate can assess (1) the compatibility of

---

[3] Also called **criteria statements** or **competency statements**.

[4] My thanks to Art Worth of Worth Developing, Largo, Florida, consultant and author of *Competency User Manual*, for introducing me to the "Meets the standard–Does not meet the standard–Exceeds the standard" concept. He has freed me forever from words such as superior, meritorious, average, and, worst of all...below average.

Job Responsibility	Performance Standard
DEVELOPS DISCHARGE PLANS FOR FAMILIES AND PATIENTS.	1. uses knowledge of patient and hospital records to prepare discharge plan 2. uses knowledge of hospital and community service agencies to develop the plan and make referrals 3. develops discharge plan with physician consultation as needed 4. counsels and/or teaches patient and family on implementing the discharge plan
MAINTAINS SENSITIVITY TO THE PERSONAL NEEDS OF OTHERS.	1. listens carefully and can restate the speaker's position on a given issue 2. describes the impact of decisions on those individuals who will be affected 3. demonstrates support and respect for others and their views, actively listening to others talk without interrupting and responding appropriately 4. addresses others tactfully on sensitive issues
PLANS AND COORDINATES THE UNIT WORKLOAD, ORGANIZING TO MAXIMIZE UTILIZATION OF RESOURCES.	1. details plan for accomplishing unit goals 2. budgets, allocates staff as per budget and classified hours per modality (HPM) 3. sets priorities as per goal plan, reviewing periodically for revision 4. defines targets and establishes a control system with verifiable measures for manager evaluation 5. monitors, comparing actual results to target, and takes corrective action as needed 6. communicates at each of the above steps to ensure clarity and purpose
SUPPORTS UNIT COST-CONTAINMENT GOALS.	1. records all patient charges during the shift used 2. completes patient care assignment within the 8-hour shift or confers with the manager as soon as an overload is apparent 3. meets annual departmental attendance standards: 　_0_ absences without notification 　_4_ late/tardy occurrences 　_4_ excused absences (1 major illness = 1 incidence)

their clinical practice philosophies and (2) the potential for agreement on or support of, organizational and management goals. If the candidate accepts the position, he or she will enter into the new position with documented knowledge of the manager's expectations, thereby giving the new union the best chance for success and longevity.

3. The manager can then use either the job description and/or the corresponding performance evaluation as a written contractual agreement to confirm and document the prehiring agreement, giving one copy to the employee and including a copy in the new employee's personnel file.

4. Advance knowledge of what to expect from a job can significantly reduce the incidence of unpleasant and conflict-producing surprises after the employee is hired. With this approach, the manager and the new employee have an opportunity, before the hire, to clarify organizational goals, to review the employee's personal goals, and assess organizational and personal goals for compatibility.

Prehiring Agreement: Skill Level

Performance standards are also helpful in rating applicants for their starting salary rate and can help control the budget by paying increased dollars only when increased responsibilities are ensured. When hiring, the goal is to offer a position and salary commensurate with the stated level of performance. Skills do vary, however, and one "experienced" professional may have significantly different experiences than another. Performance standards and corresponding skill checklists can help define the individual's experiences, skills, and knowledge of the specialty to determine a fair and appropriate beginning salary that is compatible with the salaries of those already working within the system.

Prehiring Agreement: Orientation

Orientation costs are another area of potential cost savings and budget control emanating from a good performance appraisal system. Several issues should be considered in relation to controlling orientation costs. First, each turnover of a position generates an orientation cost that varies according to the skill level of the newly hired employee. Thus, reducing turnover can also reduce orientation costs.

Second, negotiating orientation costs at the time of hiring can be a positive cost-control method. Given that the orientation will provide sufficient time for new staff members to become comfortable in their position, based on their stated skill level, it could also carry a cost limit. For example, new employees who achieved their targeted performance standards within the designated orientation time would be paid for 100 percent of their orientation salary; but those who took twice as long to do so might only be paid for 50 percent (or some other negotiated figure), thus encouraging achievement rather than failure.

Third, new graduate orientation, which may last from 4 weeks to 4 months, is another area that can benefit budgetarily from prehiring agreements based on job descriptions and/or performance evaluations. The length of orientation depends on the institution, chosen shift and specialty area, and the amount of expected responsibility. Performance standards can identify when the new employee is ready to work independently, and may even be sooner than the preplanned orientation period.

Traditionally in healthcare organizations the financial responsibility of paying full salary to the orientee has been assumed; but, because of current cost constraints, in some institutions other alternatives might have to be considered. One alternative is cost sharing by the employee and/or the technical/professional school. For example, a new graduate respiratory therapist or laboratory technician may require a longer orientation period to be competent to provide care to ICU patients. Because the extensive knowledge base required for working with patients in the ICU may not be provided for in the technical school curricula, those schools might be willing to assume or share the additional costs involved in placing and training new graduates in these areas. Another option is to include a portion of orientees' hours as part of the direct care hours allocated to the shift on which they work. Doing so will not change the actual work that they accomplish, but it would provide some documentation that they participated in a revenue-producing activity and the direct care HPM would be reflected more accurately.

Prehiring agreements can take any form, depending on the desire of the management team, provided that incoming staff, currently employed staff, and management are satisfied with the fairness and validity of the system. **Prehire Agreement & Documentation**, Form 5.2-Example, is one format that can be used to document an agreement with a new employee, in writing. By using the job description as a resource, new employees can self-evaluate, compare their actual level of performance to the evaluation criteria, and, then, identify those areas that need improvement. The first job responsibility shown on page 56, discharge planning, is used as an example to demonstrate how the form is used. Areas that do not meet the standard are prioritized, with target dates for further development and accomplishment. The target dates vary, depending on the need for the skill. When immediate expertise is essential, the department manager might even

Prehire Agreement & Documentation

Employee _____

Area of Performance That Did Not Meet the Standard	Expected Results	Corrective Action To Be Taken	Target Date
Development of the discharge plan for patients and families.	*Employee will meet the stated performance standard or achieve skill proficiency in the following areas:* * *1. Become familiar with patient and hospital records, hospital and community service agencies, and the process of consulting with physicians.* *2. Use all of the above information to develop the discharge plan and make referrals.* *3. Possess ability to counsel and/or teach patient and family how to implement the discharge plan.*	*1. Orient 2 hours in medical records department.* *2. Attend a half-day discharge planning workshop.* *3. Review all discharge planning policies and procedures.* *4. Initiate and complete an entire discharge planning process under the observation of a preceptor for the purpose of evaluation.*	*End of orientation period.*

Employee's Signature _____ Manager's Signature _____

Form 5.2-Example

* This can be footnoted to the job description and performance evaluation, and restated here for documentation purposes.

Prehire Agreement & Documentation

Employee _____

Area of Performance That Did Not Meet the Standard	Expected Results	Corrective Action To Be Taken	Target Date

Employee's Signature _____

Manager's Signature _____

Form 5.2

require that the new employee meet all of the criteria statements of the performance evaluation before the end of orientation or, even, before hiring.

Prehiring agreements are negotiations; and, if negotiated carefully and fairly, both management and the new employee will have a similar vision of what is expected to be accomplished. Because the job description describes duties and responsibilities of the employee, and the performance standards describe criteria that will be used to evaluate performance, the combination of the two becomes, and provides, both a valuable measure for, and a commitment to, prehiring agreements that are consistent with other ongoing staff agreements. Plus, the benefits to the client, the employee, and management continue after hiring.

In summary, the budget control benefits of the performance appraisal system are threefold:

1. As a prehiring tool, the performance appraisal system can be used as a self-assessment measure and as a commitment from new employees that they can meet an acceptable level of performance.

2. As an ongoing management tool, the performance appraisal system continues to provide incentives that motivate staff to achieve organizational goals and to work concurrently toward personal achievement.

3. Employees who know what is expected, and how to meet that expectation, are usually satisfied and tend to have positive performance evaluations. They tend to be employed for the long term, which reduces expensive turnover and orientation costs. Finally, they can have the incentive, via their performance appraisal system, to look within their department to discover what can be done better for the sake of quality and what can be done faster to enhance productivity.

Section 6

Prescheduling Staff: More Planning Ahead

Prescheduling—The Last Plan

Prescheduling and planning ahead for daily staffing of personnel is probably the most important challenge facing healthcare managers today. If managers are to achieve the staffing goals set forth in their budget plan, they must take appropriate action throughout the fiscal year. This means being accountable for scheduling and staffing responsibilities, which begin with the development of departmental standard hours per modality (HPM) and continue with the budget process to prescheduling of staff. Prescheduling employees using this process enables the manager to maximize both quality and productivity by adequately preparing ahead for the unknown volume and the intensity of future patient or service requirements. Prescheduling, through the preparation of time sheets for staff schedules and the daily reallocation of staff to meet classified care requirements of that day, must satisfy three diverse, but equally important, criteria: (1) Quality of patient care, (2) cost containment (or budgetary constraints), and (3) staff preference.

Quality of Patient Care

The quality of patient care, or of the service provided, can directly and indirectly contribute to a patient's condition, recovery, and satisfaction. High quality care should be the goal of every individual working in a healthcare organization. In the past we assessed quality according to the time we expended; i.e., the more time we spent with patients, the higher the quality of care we were delivering. With competition, reimbursement reductions, and serious healthcare labor shortages tightening our resource availability, it is more important than ever to identify quality goals, to determine the most effective way to achieve them, and to ensure adequate staffing levels for variable acuity and volume.

67

Cost Containment

Cost containment is no longer a voluntary option. Just a few years ago a department manager could identify the average acuity and HPM needed and budget the dollars for those hours for the upcoming fiscal year. Today, HPM are often determined by the organization as a result of financial distress, budgetary constraints, or government controls. In addition, traditional third party payers, health maintenance organizations (HMOs), and preferred provider organizations (PPOs) are also limiting care hour availability to patients as they negotiate for deep discounts and reduced payments for services. What has resulted is a decrease in revenue for patient care and, at the same time, an increase in patient care HPM requirements, patient expectations, and personnel salaries. In today's healthcare market, providers have a limited amount of money to use for the delivery of patient care. Successful healthcare managers and administrators will be the ones who are able (1) to contain costs at the same time they are meeting, or exceeding, their prestated standards of care; and (2) to continuously improve quality within existing constraints.

Staff Preference

When sincere concern and appreciation is demonstrated to staff members by management, it is usually reciprocated when the department manager has unexpected or extraordinary needs. The level of rapport and consideration that management and the professional staff have for one another enhances the quality of care and increases productivity through the efforts of a satisfied and motivated staff working toward the achievement of organizational objectives.

Reallocation: Quality, Cost, Staff

Daily staffing decisions and reallocations must address and respond to each of the criteria above if the department is to be managed at peak effectiveness and efficiency. As the manager examines acuity and modality volume levels, he or she may find it necessary to make adjustments because of (1) increased or decreased census, (2) increased or decreased acuity, (3) unexpected staff absences, or (4) individual staff skill levels. Daily adjustments help the manager reallocate both staffing hours and labor dollars to where they are needed so the goal of optimal care at the lowest cost can be successfully pursued. Daily adjustments and reallocation of staff can work positively for both the institution and the staff members. For example, a staff member who works 7-3/3-11 on a Thursday to cover for a sick coworker, can take Friday off and have a 3-day weekend as a bonus. Careful schedule planning (i.e., prescheduling to meet the *average* acuity and *average* volume) positions the department so that quality, cost containment, and staff preference objectives will be met. It also lays the ground work for flexible and efficient reallocation decisions that will enable ongoing achievement of objectives regardless of unexpected variations in volume and acuity.

Preplanning, Preparation, Process

Prescheduling and daily staffing of personnel can be the bane of a manager's existence; or it can be a fair, efficient, and cost-effective system designed to meet the needs of the patients, staff, and administration. Thoughtful planning and preparation before the actual scheduling process can help ensure optimal results.

Staffing System Planning Process

- Organizational and departmental objectives should focus on meeting the needs of the patients, staff members, and budget.

- The primary objective of a department is to provide a prestated standard of care and performance within a target amount of time, for each modality.

- Dollars required to provide the following become the department salary budget:

    (1) Direct hours per modality (HPM)
    (2) Nonproductive hours
    (3) Fixed hours

- Unit goals, including the desired HPM, are approved when required budget dollars are approved and allocated.

- Unit goals should be clearly prioritized and communicated. Circumstances that would change priorities should be included in the communication.

- Personnel and staffing policies must support organizational objectives, be mutually agreed to by all involved, and be communicated verbally and/or in writing.

Personnel and Staffing Policies

Policies for staffing and scheduling of personnel provide the backbone of successful staffing systems that ensure fair treatment, adequate coverage for patient care requirements, and cost-effective scheduling. Although policies for each institution must be developed and implemented to meet the individual needs of that institution, some common policy subjects are discussed below.

Sample Staffing Policies

- All personnel will have 26 weekends off per year. Whenever possible, those weekends off will follow an every-other-weekend pattern.

- All requests will be granted in the order received, with the earliest dated request given priority. Exceptions:
    (1) Emergency medical leave
    (2) Winter holidays:
        - Every employee will be off the Christmas **or** New Year's holiday.
        - Whatever holiday is worked one year will be guaranteed off the next year.
        - Trades will be approved by the department manager after everyone has been scheduled for at least one holiday off.

- All changes of scheduled days are to be written, approved, and signed by the manager and turned into the staffing clerk. Changes requiring overtime (or additional overtime) will not be approved.

- Specific weekdays off can be guaranteed if the employee works every weekend.

- Once schedules are posted (2 weeks prior to the start of the period), no changes will be made without the permission of the employee.

- All summer vacation requests must be submitted to the manager by March 15. Approvals will be returned no later than April 15.

Once policies are agreed on,[5] written, and communicated to all staff through departmental meetings and pre-employment interviews, they serve as a reference for all staffing-related decisions and provide guidelines for equal treatment of all employees. Further, the staffing policies are useful employee references that outline what is expected from the employee and, as important, what the employee can expect and count on from management.

> *Staffing policies take time to develop—*
> *especially when you get staff actively involved*
> *in the decision-making process.*
> *But having fair, consistent policies that support both*
> *organizational and individual staff goals makes*
> *their development more than worth the effort.*

Planning Ahead for Vacations and Other Prescheduled Absences

Requests for vacation, and other special requests for time off, is another area that should be considered before preparing the time schedules, if there is to be a balance among the needs of patients, staff, and budget. The vacation scheduling memoranda—**Vacation Notice**, Form 6.1; **Vacation Memo**, Form 6.2; and **Request for Days Off**, Form 6.3 (on the pages that follow)—are all useful formats that will be valuable to the individual responsible for preparing schedules. For the manager, planning ahead can make the difference between frustration and sanity. If the manager has all the requests in hand when preparing the schedules, he or she can arrange the schedule so that all reasonable requests can be granted. If a request comes in at the last minute, after other coworkers' days off have been promised, the manager can only refer the individual to coworkers for a trade, or call off in the event of an unexpected low census.

---

[5] Staff ad hoc (or "self-destruct" committees) are an excellent methodology for developing or revising staffing policies. Also, it is a good idea to have each employee sign a copy of the staffing policies. One copy should remain in the personnel file, and the other copy should be retained by the employee for future reference.

Vacation Notice

Date: _____

To: Department Staff Members

From: Department Manager

Subject: Vacation Scheduling

As of _____ you are eligible for _____ vacation days, to be taken any time
        Date   *Number*

within this fiscal year beginning _____ and ending _____ . Please consult
                                  Start Date   *End Date*

your personnel handbook to double-check my calculations; and, if you have ques-

tions, call me at extension number _____ . It is your responsibility to keep track of

your vacation days and review your paycheck stub for proper payment; but I'll be

glad to double-check your remaining vacation time.   Summer (May-September)

vacation requests must be submitted by March 15. All other vacation requests should

be submitted 6 - 8 weeks in advance.

_____
Department Manager's Signature

Form 6.1

Vacation Memo

February 15

To: *Department Staff Members*

From: *Department Manager*

Subject: *Vacation Scheduling*

1. Vacation requests must be submitted to me 6-8 weeks in advance, or by March 15 for summer (May–September) vacations. Summer leave of absence (time off without pay) requests by employees who have not yet earned vacation are also due by March 15. Summer vacations requested by March 15 will be approved, in writing, by April 15.

*2. Requests must be submitted on **Request for Days Off**, Form 6.3 (shown on page 74), and written on the **Vacation Schedule**, Form 6.4 (shown on pages 76-77), which is posted on the department bulletin board.*

*3. If there are too many vacation requests for the same time, the individual with the latest date on his or her request (i.e., first come, first serve) will be contacted, and an attempt will be made to plan another acceptable date. The best way to avoid a conflict, in advance, is to review the **Vacation Schedule** to see what has already been requested and approved. No more than two vacations can be approved at the same time.*

4. Changes in an approved vacation require that a written request be submitted to me. It will be processed as a new request.

5. After all vacation requests are processed, employees who are eligible for vacation and have not submitted a request will be contacted and an available time will be suggested. If the employee has no preference, an assignment will be made that is agreeable to the employee and compatible with the department's staffing needs.

6. Advance vacation pay requests are due 4 weeks before start of vacation.

7. Please keep in mind that vacation scheduling may affect the way your weekends are scheduled, but not their total number.

Request for Days Off

Unit: _____

Name/Position: _____   Date: _____

Day/Date(s) of Requested Time Off[1]: _____

Pay:
_____ Sick Hours[2]   _____ Regular Day Off
_____ Vacation Hours   _____ Holiday Hours

_____ Other (Jury Duty, Military, Death, Medical, Personal Leave)
Describe _____

If this request involves your normal weekend to work and you have made arrangements with a coworker to trade weekends, please ask coworker to sign here _____ .

[1] If you have a preference of how benefit days are to be scheduled, indicate here _____ and describe on the back of this form.
[2] Sick time may be prescheduled if the physician request is on file in the Health Office.

Policy Issues: Requests for Days Off

- Encourage staff to plan as far ahead as possible to facilitate approval of their requests.

- Require requests be submitted before the time schedule is started. After that time a trade will have to be made with a coworker.

- Grant requests in the order they are received.

- Encourage or require staff to submit vacation requests, especially for summer vacation, well in advance to enable staff to coordinate their approved vacation with their family.

- Notify staff as soon as possible about the outcome of their requests.

- Keep records of requested days off, including those not granted, and of employees who have had special holidays off. Monitor request activity and fairness of the requests.

- Take notice of staff members who never ask for any days off. Make sure they are getting some special holidays and their choice of days off once in a while.

- If the request cannot be granted, look for a negotiation or a partial granting and discuss it with the individual.

- Keep in mind that (even with a manager's best effort) not every request can be granted.

Vacation Schedule

Fiscal Year _____

Department _Engineering_

Month	Jan	Feb	Mar	Apr	May	June	July	Aug	Sept	Oct	Nov	Dec
Week Beginning:	3 10 17 24 31	7 14 21 28	6 13 20 27	3 10 17 24	1 8 15 22 29	5 12 19 26	3 10 17 24 31	7 14 21 28	4 11 18 25	2 9 16 23 30	6 13 20 27	4 11 18 25
Employee:												
J. Jones	a											
T. Kirk		a										
D. Blair							a					
C. Todaro									a			
R. Johnson			a			a						
Y. Kieval								a				
N. Sterling					a							
B. Meyer												a
W. Lands				a						a		
D. Russell			a					?				
K. Victor											a	
H. Hoesing										a		
D. Kranz												?

Legend:
a = approved
? = pending

Form 6.4-Example

Vacation Schedule

Department _____

Fiscal Year _____

Month	Jan	Feb	Mar	Apr	May	June	July	Aug	Sept	Oct	Nov	Dec
Week Beginning:												
Employee:												

Form 6.4

Scheduling earned benefit time should be respected and acknowledged as something special, giving full effort to granting an employee's first or second choice for time off. Employees work hard to earn 2 to 3 weeks off with their families, and giving priority to vacation time is one way to demonstrate good will and appreciation in the organization. With careful planning by both management and staff, this becomes an attainable goal and can usually be achieved without compromising patient care or cost containment goals. You should grant the approval in writing with a form, such as **Vacation Approval**, Form 6.5, and keep a copy in your current request file so you don't forget to schedule it when the time arrives.

Basic Scheduling Techniques

Prescheduling employees through the preparation of time sheets is a time-consuming task, but it can also be extremely satisfying …when you're finished…and sometimes it can even be fun. The following section is written so that a novice can use it to learn this skill, but even seasoned managers will pick up an idea or two and can use this as a reference for teaching new managers.   Here is a list of the information that the manager should know *in advance* of preparing schedules:

Prescheduling Information to Know

- Standard of care: Budgeted direct care hours per modality (HPM)

- Staffing pattern for the average projected census and approved staffing mix (number of professionals, technicians, clerks, etc.)

- Staffing policies

- Skill levels of staff: Ability for relief charge, years of experience, etc.

- Number of days that part-time personnel work per week

- Availability of per diem personnel: How much they'll work and when

- Individual staff idiosyncracies: With this knowledge, schedules can be given a personal touch and meet everyone's needs more often. For example, if Jan asks for every Monday off to volunteer at her child's school, maybe she'd prefer to cover 3-11 on Mondays so she could save her day off for herself.

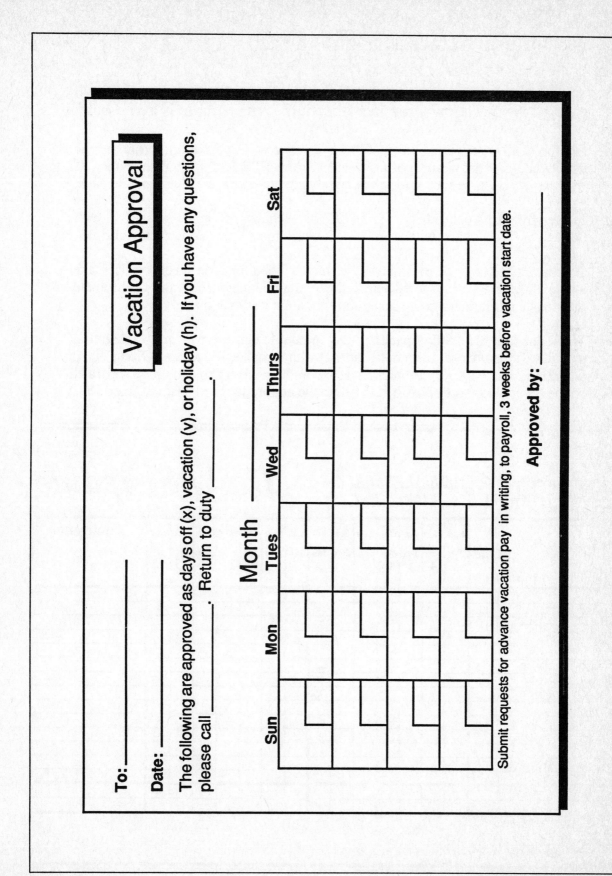

Vacation Approval

To: _____

Date: _____

The following are approved as days off (x), vacation (v), or holiday (h). If you have any questions, please call _____. Return to duty _____.

Month _____

Sun	Mon	Tues	Wed	Thurs	Fri	Sat

Submit requests for advance vacation pay in writing, to payroll, 3 weeks before vacation start date.

Approved by: _____

The Scheduling Process, Step-by-Step

Once prescheduling information (page 78) is known, the task of scheduling can be simplified if you follow a routine procedure. An example is given below.

1. On the **Daily Schedule**, Form 6.6 (a 2-week staff schedule), write in the employee's (1) name and position, and (2) the FTE hours hired to work. If working with a large unit, it may be desirable to put each shift on a separate page.

2. Indicate regular weekend off with an "X" on each day off, and weekend on with dashes "—" (...a pencil with an eraser is always recommended for scheduling).

3. If an employee (e.g., D. Blair) is on the weekend that the time sheet begins, make a note of the last day off (noted here in the Sunday, January 3 column) to eliminate the chance of unintentionally scheduling too long a stretch on duty.

4. Work done on the staffing pattern development is carried over in prescheduling actual staff members to meet both patient volume and acuity needs. Direct, fixed, and nonproductive FTEs are broken down on the pattern and should be separated on the schedule as well. F. Albert is filling the nonproductive FTE, and fixed FTEs

---

Department & Shift <u>PHYSICAL THERAPY: 7-3</u>   **Daily Schedule**
Payroll Period Ending   <u>JANUARY 16</u>

Name	Position	FTE	Sun Jan 3	Mon Jan 4	Tue Jan 5	Wed Jan 6	Thu Jan 7	Fri Jan 8	Sat Jan 9	Sun Jan 10	Mon Jan 11	Tue Jan 12	Wed Jan 13	Thu Jan 14	Fri Jan 15	Sat Jan 16	Comments
J. Jones	7-3/RPT	1.0	X						—	—						X	
D. Blair	7-3/RPT	1.0	—ᵂ						X	X						—	
C. Todaro	7-3/RPT	1.0	—ᵀᴴ						X	X						—	
N. Lee	7-3/RPT	.5	X						—	—						—	
V. Hart	7-3/RPT	.5	—ᶠ						X	X						X	
Y. Kieval	7-3/RPT	.2	X						X	X						X	
B. Rink	7-3/PT Aide	1.0	X						—	—						X	
E. Mack	7-3/PT Aide	.4	—ᵂ						X	X						—	
F. Albert	NP/PT Aide	.6	X						—	—						X	
TOTALS (5.6 + .6 NP =) 6.2			4						4	4						4	

Schedule Building: Step 1

have been omitted entirely for this exercise.[6] This action serves as a reminder (a) to schedule benefit time each pay period and (b) to diminish the urge to add the non-productive or fixed hours into the direct care hours, which would reduce available hours for vacation, holiday coverage, and indirect care. Although F. Albert is covering a weekend (January 9 and 10), which is not benefit time, the per diem employee, Y. Kieval, will end up covering the two additional benefit days. Note: N. Lee and V. Hart traded weekends on January 16 to accommodate Hart's vacation.

5. Make a note in the "Comments" section of the benefit time due to be taken as a reminder to the employee and the person completing the schedules.

6. Write in all requests for time off, or on, or to work on other shifts with an "R" (i.e., X^R, —^{R}, 11-7^R) as a reminder to all that this is a request. If holidays and vacation days are occasionally assigned, then requested ones should also be marked with an "R" so that it is not forgotten when the schedules are being prepared, and also it reminds the manager during the period that these are special days off and not to call for extra shift coverage. Assume at this point that all requests can be granted,

---

Department & Shift <u>*PHYSICAL THERAPY: 7-3*</u>   *Daily Schedule*
Payroll Period Ending <u>*JANUARY 16*</u>

Name	Position	FTE	Sun Jan 3	Mon Jan 4	Tue Jan 5	Wed Jan 6	Thu Jan 7	Fri Jan 8	Sat Jan 9	Sun Jan 10	Mon Jan 11	Tue Jan 12	Wed Jan 13	Thu Jan 14	Fri Jan 15	Sat Jan 16	Comments
J. Jones	7-3/RPT	1.0	X					—	—							X	HOLIDAY
D. Blair	7-3/RPT	1.0	—^{W}					X^R	X^R	HOL^R						—	~~HOLIDAY~~ (REQUESTED 12/1)
C. Todaro	7-3/RPT	1.0	—TH			X^R	VAC^R	X^R	X^R							—	(REQUESTED 11/2)
N. Lee	7-3/RPT	.5	X	11-7	X^R	X^R		—	—							—	ON 2 WEEKENDS, OFF 2
V. Hart	7-3/RPT	.5	—^{F}	X	X^R	X^R	X^R	VAC^R	X^R	X^R	X^R	X^R	VAC^R	VAC^R	VAC^R	X^R	OFF 2 WEEKENDS, ON 2
Y. Kieval	7-3/RPT	.2	X		X^R	3-11^R	X^R		X	X						X	PER DIEM
B. Rink	7-3/PT Aide	1.0	X					—	—							X	3 VACATION DAYS LEFT
E. Mack	7-3/PT Aide	.4	—^{W}					X	X							—	
F. Albert	NP/PT Aide	.6	X					—	—							X	NONPRODUCTIVE
TOTALS (5.6 + .6 NP =)	6.2		4					4	4							4	

Schedule Building: Step 2

---

[6] Note that this example does not follow the example on pages 40-42 as the large number of FTEs involved would make it more complicated.

but also make a note in the "Comments" section of the request date (shown in the example below as "12/1" and "11/2") in case requests for the time off are more plentiful than the available time.

7. If staff need to be rotated to another shift to cover a key vacancy, do it at this point so they can have a preference for days off. Some 7-3 staff, for example, like their day off the day before, rather than after, rotating to 3-ll, their rationale being that if they're tired the following day, they'd rather be at work. At times shift rotation is mandatory.[7] The person preparing the schedule cannot change that fact, but he or she can make the chore as pleasant, or as palatable, as possible. Note also that by the time the schedules are done, the per diem Registered Physical Therapist (RPT) will be working 2 days to cover benefit time and 2 extra days to cover the hours required to cover vacant positions on other shifts.

8. Start by giving the remaining staff their days off and leave the part-time staff for last, because their days are more flexible. Keep counting as you move along,

---

Daily Schedule

Department & Shift __PHYSICAL THERAPY: 7-3__
Payroll Period Ending __JANUARY 16__

Name	Position	FTE	Sun Jan 3	Mon Jan 4	Tue Jan 5	Wed Jan 6	Thu Jan 7	Fri Jan 8	Sat Jan 9	Sun Jan 10	Mon Jan 11	Tue Jan 12	Wed Jan 13	Thu Jan 14	Fri Jan 15	Sat Jan 16	Comments
J. Jones	7-3/RPT	1.0	X	—	—	—	—	X	—	—	—	—	X	—	—	X	HOLIDAY
D. Blair	7-3/RPT	1.0	—W	X	—	—	—	—	X^R	X^R	HOL^R	—	—	—	X	—	~~HOLIDAY~~ (REQUESTED 12/1)
C. Todaro	7-3/RPT	1.0	—TH	—	—	—	X^R	VAC^R	X^R	X^R	—	—	—	X	—	—	(REQUESTED 11/2)
N. Lee	7-3/RPT	.5	X	11-7	X^R	X^R	—	X	—	—	X	X	X	X	X	—	ON 2 WEEKENDS, OFF 2
V. Hart	7-3/RPT	.5	—F	X	X^R	X^R	X^R	VAC^R	X^R	X^R	X^R	X^R	VAC^R	VAC^R	VAC^R	X^R	OFF 2 WEEKENDS, ON 2
Y. Kieval	7-3/RPT	.2	X	—	X^R	3-11^H	X^R	—	X	X	—	X	X	X	X	X	PER DIEM
B. Rink	7-3/PT Aide	1.0	X	—	—	—	X	—	—	—	—	X	—	—	—	X	3 VACATION DAYS LEFT
E. Mack	7-3/PT Aide	.4	—W	X	X	—	X	X	X	X	—	X	X	X	X	—	
F. Albert	NP/PT Aide	.6	X	X	X	X	—	—	—	—	X	X	—	—	—	X	NONPRODUCTIVE
TOTALS (5.6 + .6 NP =)		6.2	4	4	4	4	4	4	4	4	4	4	4	4	4	4	

Schedule Building: Step 3

---

[7] If rotations are needed or, for that matter, if any other unpleasant assignments are required, make sure assignments are fair and equitable. Even if staff members trade 11-7s for weekends off, *let them make the trade after the schedules are posted.* The posted schedules should always demonstrate absolute equality for rotations, floats, etc., and records should be kept to document assignments.

making sure continuity is maintained for the number of staff, staff mix, and skill levels. Prescheduling four staff members daily allows sufficient staff to react quickly to (1) high or low volume and (2) high or low acuity. A day when only 3 are prescheduled will inevitably be the day both volume and acuity skyrocket. Then the manager will be searching for two additional employees, instead of one.

9. Review individually with staff any time changes are made that are out of the ordinary, such as a change in routine weekend off or a change in a routine rotation to another shift.

10. Finally, post schedules at least 2 weeks before the start of the period. Be available for comments, corrections, and so forth; and, if you do make an error, admit it and fix it!

Adjustments should be made to complement individual personnel policies and routines of the specific departments involved. Success depends on communication, fairness, and adherence to both the budget and quality assurance goals. It is equally important that cost guidelines and the desired level of patient care not be compromised as a result of responding to staff preference.

Priorities and Scheduling

As discussed earlier in the section, prescheduling must satisfy three criteria: (1) quality of care, (2) cost containment, and (3) staff preference. None can stand alone. It isn't enough to deliver high quality care, when it is so expensive that it creates financial problems for the organization, or staff are miserable because they are working 3 weekends a month. It may seem great for a while, but sooner or later the financial burden will be felt or staff will begin to find new jobs at other organizations. On the other hand, it isn't enough to make big bucks, when patients are complaining and waiting for procedures in hallways, and the employees are complaining about overload.

But it also is not realistic to expect to meet all of these goals, all the time; so it is best that managers at all levels in an organization (1) identify and agree on the priorities of the organization; (2) agree on when exceptions should and should not be made; and (3) discuss whether priorities should be decided at the departmental level or organizationwide. Even the most cost-conscious manager needs the flexibility to make a decision that may not be the most cost effective, but that will allow one of the other goals of patient care or staff preference to be met successfully. Although sound planning provides the basis for effective allocation of staff, the manager must use judgment and experience to set priorities and make decisions. Some examples are discussed on the next page.

It's OK To Be Flexible

The manager may preschedule less staff during the summer months to accommodate more vacation scheduling, as long as other staff agree to carry the extra load in the event of an unexpected high census.

The manager may elect to staff short over the winter holiday season when a predictably low census is expected.

On selected days, when department projects, policies, or planning activities are scheduled, the manager may preschedule extra staff. If this is planned for properly, it can be achieved without compromising budget targets.

Scheduling Exercise

Though rare, staff members occasionally make unreasonable requests. Also, sometimes managers get the idea that their employees don't understand or appreciate the agony they go through to complete a schedule. If either of these scenarios matches your situation, or if you just want to brush up on your scheduling technique, give the **Scheduling Exercise** on the next page a try. One set of answers is on page 86. There are many different potential outcomes, so don't worry if your answers don't match. If you follow the *Scheduling Exercise Rules,* the exercise is more difficult; and, as seasoned managers already know, putting real names and faces on those positions makes scheduling even more of a challenge. Give it to your own staff members too and then sit back and watch what unfolds. Some staff members decide they like being involved in their schedules and may even opt to do their own schedules to have more autonomy. This is fine as long as they understand that along with the increased control comes responsibility for coverage. Other staff members want no part of the scheduling process, and that's fine too; but giving them a chance to experience doing the schedules will enlighten them about the importance and complexity of this responsibility.

Daily Schedule

Department & Shift ___ADMITTING - all shifts___

Payroll Period Ending ___JANUARY 16___

Scheduling Exercise Rules

- "X"s cannot be changed.
- Target: 4 scheduled daily, 3 on weekends.
- Use part time staff no more than budgeted FTE hours.
- Avoid more than 4 days on duty between single days off.
- Staff rotated to cover other shifts must have the next day off.
- Indicate "on-duty" days with dashes (–).
- Remember those are people you're moving around... not just Xs & dashes!

Name	Position	FTE	Sun Jan 3	Mon Jan 4	Tue Jan 5	Wed Jan 6	Thu Jan 7	Fri Jan 8	Sat Jan 9	Sun Jan 10	Mon Jan 11	Tue Jan 12	Wed Jan 13	Thu Jan 14	Fri Jan 15	Sat Jan 16	Comments
1A	7-3/Clerk	1.0	X^R					X^R					X^R			X^R	
1B	7-3/Clerk	1.0							X^R	X^R							
1C	7-3/Clerk	1.0	X^R													X^R	
1D	7-3/Clerk	1.0			X^R	X^R						X^R	X^R				
1E	7-3/Clerk	1.0							X^R	X^R							
1F	7-3/Clerk	.6							X^R	X^R	3-11^R						
	TOTALS	5.6	3	4	4	4	4	4	3	3	4	4	4	4	4	3	
2A	3-11/Clerk	1.0	X^R													X^R	
2B	3-11/Clerk	1.0							X^R	X^R							
2C	3-11/Clerk	1.0	X^R													X^R	
2D	3-11/Clerk	1.0							X^R	X^R	HOL^R						
2E	3-11/Clerk	.5	X^R						X^R	X^R							
2F	3-11/Clerk	.5															
2G	Unfilled	.6									①4						
	TOTALS	5.6	3	4	4	4	4	4	3	3	4	4	4	4	4	3	
3A	11-7/Clerk	1.0	X^R												X^R		
3B	11-7/Clerk	1.0							X^R	X^R							
3C	11-7/Clerk	1.0	X^R													X^R	
3D	11-7/Clerk	1.0							X^R	X^R							
3E	11-7/Clerk	1.0			X^R	X^R					X^R						On 2 weekends, off 2
3F	11-7/Clerk	.6	X^R	X^R	VAC^R	VAC^R	VAC^R	X^R	X^R	X^R							Off 2 weekends, on 2
	TOTALS	5.6	3	4	4	4	4	4	3	3	4	4	4	4	4	3	

Form 6.6-Exercise

Daily Schedule

Department & Shift ___ADMITTING - all shifts___
Payroll Period Ending ___JANUARY 16___

Name	Position	FTE	Sun Jan 3	Mon Jan 4	Tue Jan 5	Wed Jan 6	Thu Jan 7	Fri Jan 8	Sat Jan 9	Sun Jan 10	Mon Jan 11	Tue Jan 12	Wed Jan 13	Thu Jan 14	Fri Jan 15	Sat Jan 16	Comments
1A	7-3/Clerk	1.0	X^R	–	–	–	–	X^R	–	–	–	–	X^R	–	–	X^R	
1B	7-3/Clerk	1.0	–	X	–	–	–	–	X^R	–	–	–	–	X	X	–	
1C	7-3/Clerk	1.0	X^R	–	–	X^R	X	–	–	–	X	–	–	–	HOL	X^R	
1D	7-3/Clerk	1.0	–	–	X^R	X^R	–	–	X^R	X^R	X^R	X^R	X^R	–	–	–	
1E	7-3/Clerk	1.0	–	–	11-7	X	–	HOL	X^R	X^R	3-11^R	–	–	X	–	–	
1F	7-3/Clerk	.6	X	X	–	–	X	–	X^R	X^R	X	X	–	X	–	X	
	TOTALS	5.6	3	4	4	4	4	4	3	3	4	4	4	4	4	3	
2A	3-11/Clerk	1.0	X^R	–	–	–	–	X	–	–	–	–	X	–	–	X^R	If there had not been
2B	3-11/Clerk	1.0	–	X	–	–	–	–	X^R	X^R	–	–	–	X	–	–	extra staff members
2C	3-11/Clerk	1.0	X^R	–	–	–	–	X	–	–	–	X	–	–	–	X^R	on 11-7, the part-time
2D	3-11/Clerk	1.0	–	–	X	X	X	–	X^R	X^R HOL^R	HOL^R	–	–	X	X	–	staff could have been
2E	3-11/Clerk	.5	X^R	X	X	X	X	–	–	–	X	X	X	X	X	X^R	scheduled extra days
2F	3-11/Clerk	.5	–	X	–	X	X	X	X^R	X^R	X	–	–	X	X	–	(at straight pay) to
2G	Unfilled	.6	X	X	(1F)4	X	X	X	X	(1F)4	(1F)4	X	(3C)4	X	(3B)4	X	cover the 2G vacancy.
	TOTALS	5.6	3	4	4	4	4	4	3	3	4	4	4	4	4	3	
3A	11-7/Clerk	1.0	X^R	–	–	–	X	–	X^R	–	X	–	–	–	–	X^R	
3B	11-7/Clerk	1.0	–	X	–	–	–	X	X^R	X^R	–	–	–	X	3-11	–	Preferred on after 3-11
3C	11-7/Clerk	1.0	X^R	–	–	–	–	X	–	–	–	X	3-11	–	–	X^R	Preferred on after 3-11
3D	11-7/Clerk	1.0	–	–	X	–	–	X	–	–	–	–	–	X	–	–	
3E	11-7/Clerk	1.0	–	–	X^R	X^R	VAC^R	–	–	X^R	X^R	–	–	–	–	X^R	On 2 weekends, off 2
3F	11-7/Clerk	.6	X^R	X^R	VAC^R	VAC^R	VAC^R	X^R	X^R	X^R	–	X	–	X	X	–	Off 2 weekends, on 2
	TOTALS	5.6	3	4	4	4	4	4	3	3	4	4	4	4	4	3	

Form 6.6-Exercise Answer & Example

Daily Schedule

Department & Shift _____

Payroll Period Ending _____

Name	Position	FTE	Sun	Mon	Tue	Wed	Thu	Fri	Sat	Sun	Mon	Tue	Wed	Thu	Fri	Sat	Comments
		Day															
		Date															

Form 6.6

Section 7

Making Schedules Flexible

Scheduling as a Recruitment & Retention Tool

Staffing has a lot more to do with quality than just scheduling employees to be on the right shift on the right day. If there aren't enough personnel hired and scheduled to provide the budgeted hours per modality, the employees who are scheduled won't be able to deliver the target standard of care, regardless of the sophistication level of management's staffing systems or techniques. Staffing and scheduling practices of a department have an enormous impact on recruitment and retention, which, in turn, affect quality in the care and services we provide.

There are several potential repercussions that can occur when a department manager is unable to hire enough personnel to fill budgeted (and volume-required) positions. One, there are fewer available personnel to schedule, which reduces flexibility to accommodate requests for time off. Two, staff become tired and dissatisfied because they are working short staffed (with a greater workload), working extra shifts, or can't get the time off they requested. Three, when there are not enough available hours, staff members are placed in the position of having to either rush or delete components of care or the service they provided...which has the potential of compromising quality. If an employee only has 30 minutes to do a modality or task, which, according to the standard, requires an hour, something has got to give. Healthcare professionals don't take these events lightly; and many have left well-paying jobs, and even their professions, rather than participate in providing what they perceive to be less than optimal care.

There are a lot of positive actions managers can take to prepare and help their staff deal with these situations, as we discussed in the early part of the book; but, at the same time, they must continue to address and resolve the underlying root problem of vacant positions. In today's healthcare market, this is no simple task. Already scarce labor resources are being courted away by home care, outpatient and ambulatory care centers, physician practices, third party payers, and even other professions. Although the nursing profession has gotten a lot of well-deserved press lately regarding the acute nursing shortage, nurses are not the only ones suffering through a labor shortage. Many departments within our healthcare organizations are having as frustrating and, sometimes, as frightening a time as nursing. We can all learn from nursing's experiences, particularly in the area of flexible scheduling. Yes, flexible scheduling plans can be expensive; but, according to basic economic theory, salaries will rise in times of demand so why not be a step ahead and use those dollars (or the ones you'll save from reduced overtime, turnover costs, and absentee pay) to reward employees who work undesirable days and shifts. Most of us already do it to some extent with differential pay for less desirable shifts, so the precedent has been set. We'll talk about justifying these costs later in the section.

In times of shortage managers can make the scheduling function more effective and more efficient by meeting recruitment and retention issues head on. Healthcare workers have a variety of expectations from their positions, ranging from personal satisfaction, to intellectual challenge, to money, to compatibility with personal life style. Flexible scheduling options provide an opportunity for management to tune into their existing and potential employees needs and wants and compete for resources more successfully. They have proved to be effective and are worth consideration for implementation in your own department.

Assessing Satisfaction Levels

The best, and easiest, way to figure out what your employees want from their jobs and their schedules is simply to ask them. The **Satisfaction Questionnaire**, Form 7.1 (on the opposite page), is just one method you can use. Written surveys allow management to obtain information from a large number of employees, but you can also use individual interviews or focus groups to gather information. Asking employees what *they* want not only furnishes management with information, but also sends a strong message to employees that management cares about what they want, is aware of the shortages, and is working on a solution. A more detailed list of issues on which you might want to focus is shown on page 92.

Sometimes, managers who are buried deep in applications and recruitment efforts are surprised to discover that their employees think that management doesn't care or isn't aware, or worse, that this is management's way of getting them to work harder. When there is no communication, staff members usually assume the worst; so, when times are tough it's more critical than ever to communicate as much as possible. Even when the communication is bad news, it is better to talk

Satisfaction Questionnaire

As you know our hospital has an active recruitment and retention program. We wish to learn as much as possible about the reasons our professional staff members stay, and why they leave. We have designed this questionnaire to provide information that will help us with our recruitment and retention efforts and would appreciate your taking time to complete it (additional comments may be added on the back of form or attached). Responses will be confidential and used for statistical purposes only. If your are filling out this questionaire as part of your resignation process,* you may prefer to reserve your comments for your exit interview.

Current Position: _____   **Manager (Yes/No):** _____

Please rate the following items:

Lowest Satisfaction Level		Highest Satisfaction Level		Did this item contribute to your decision to leave (L) or stay (S)?
1	**2**	**3**		
_____	_____	_____	Salary and/or fringe benefits	_____
_____	_____	_____	Workload and responsibility level	_____
_____	_____	_____	Ability to deliver high quality care	_____
_____	_____	_____	Authority and autonomy given to you	_____
_____	_____	_____	Respect by administration	_____
_____	_____	_____	Respect by physicians	
_____	_____	_____	Communication from and/or to colleagues	_____
_____	_____	_____	Communication from and/or to superiors	_____
_____	_____	_____	Type and amount of supervision provided	_____
_____	_____	_____	Stimulation from superiors and work environment	
_____	_____	_____	Orientation and ongoing training provided	_____
_____	_____	_____	Staffing and floating practices	
_____	_____	_____	Flexibility of scheduling	_____
_____	_____	_____	Responsiveness to suggestions and complaints	_____
_____	_____	_____	Promotion opportunities (both clinical and managerial)	_____
_____	_____	_____	Responsiveness to personal needs (i.e. child care)	_____

If you are resigning, why are you leaving?

_____ Retirement   _____ Found a better position

_____ Moving out of the area   _____ Spouse transfer/move to another city

_____ Unhappy with working conditions   _____ Other _____
         described above

_____ Leaving my profession because _____

_____

_____

---

* Use this survey as an ongoing assessment tool and for exit interviews. Print on different color paper so data can be separated for analysis.

Form 7.1

with employees; sometimes their input can make a big difference. You may be trying to figure out how to justify the cost of a 24-hour weekend plan when what they really want is to work three 12-hour days per week (much less expensive plan) or just to be able to count on having every other weekend off.

Recruitment & Retention Issues

- *Treatment by management, physicians*
- *Workload and responsibility levels*
- *Work environment (physical and behavioral)*
- *Quality: Standards of care and performance*
- *Staff-to-workload ratio (budgeted & actual)*
- *Salary and fringe benefits*
- *Personnel and staffing policies*
- *Integrity of keeping scheduling promises*
- *Communication*
- *Promotion opportunities*
- *Education and development opportunities*
- *Independence and autonomy*
- *Flexibility of scheduling*
- *Staffing and floating practices*
- *Type and amount of supervision and stimulation provided by management*
- *Responsiveness to suggestions, complaints, and personal needs*

These may or may not be your issues. You can find out for sure by talking to your employees. In fact, you might even want to get a task force of employees to work with management to look into the subject of satisfaction and scheduling options. That way they can share the responsibility, some of the work that's involved in researching and justifying such a project, and, also, some of the gratification that management experiences when objectives are achieved. If objectives, guidelines, and limits are agreed on by both management and employees before the start of the project, then everyone can work together toward the most satisfying results. Here are some sample objectives.

Flexible Scheduling Task Force
Sample Objectives

• *To identify employee scheduling preferences.*

• *To research a variety of scheduling plans for cost and implementation feasibility.*

• *To recommend plans for implementation.*[8]

Evaluating Flexible Scheduling Plans

Whether or not you decide to use a task force to evaluate different flexible scheduling plans, every effort should be made to involve employees as much as possible. After all, the purpose of the analysis is to figure out how to keep them satisfied and employed in your department as well as to recruit new employees. They have a lot to gain personally and professionally, and a lot to give too, because they are the experts when it comes to what *they* want.

There are many different kinds of flexible scheduling plans. Managers working to meet the needs of their patients, or clients, have considered some diverse and unbelievable options, even bizarre ones, provided that (1) patient care, or the quality of that service delivery, benefited and (2) the plan was fair to all employees. And that's usually okay with employees. They know management doesn't have access to a magic wand; and, as a rule, they expect only that management cares about the situation and is actively pursuing a fair and equitable solution.

The **Flexible Scheduling Options Glossary** on the next page gives an overview for just a few of the plans. There are many possible ways to vary each one,

---

[8] Roey Kirk, "Nurse Task Force Guides Flexible Scheduling Program," *Hospitals,* August 16, 1981, pp. 60, 68.

Glossary
Flexible Scheduling Options

<table>
<tr>
<td>24-Hour
Weekends</td>
<td>Employees work two 12-hour shifts every weekend (7 A.M.-7 P.M. or 7 P.M.- 7 A.M.) and are off Monday through Friday. They are paid using a variety of different schemes, ultimately, to increase their hourly salary for working undesirable shifts.[9]</td>
</tr>
<tr>
<td>Weekends Off</td>
<td>Employees work five 8-hour shifts, Monday through Friday, have weekends off, and are paid for hours worked.</td>
</tr>
<tr>
<td>Variable-
Length Shifts</td>
<td>Full-time employees can choose to work six 12-hour shifts or seven 10-hour shifts in a two-week pay period. Part-time employees can choose 6-hour shifts, or 4-hour shifts, or any time length compatible with the needs of the department.</td>
</tr>
<tr>
<td>Variable
Shift Times</td>
<td>Department managers can choose to vary the traditional 7-3, 8-5, 3-11, or 11-7 schedules to provide optimal staffing during peak periods (11 A.M. to 7 P.M., for example), or as needed.</td>
</tr>
<tr>
<td>Traditional
Schedule
with Bonus</td>
<td>Employees who continue on traditional every-other-weekend rotation are paid a bonus for weekends and holidays worked. Salaried personnel, not usually eligible for overtime pay, are eligible for the bonus too.</td>
</tr>
<tr>
<td>Self-staffing</td>
<td>Department managers allow responsible employees to take control of their own schedules, within mutually agreed on staffing guidelines. One group prepared schedules for each pay period without names; then, employees, taking turns each period, would sign up for a schedule that matched their needs</td>
</tr>
</table>

---

[9] Roey Kirk, "Flexible Scheduling," *Nursing Life,* March/April 1983, pp. 32-4.

depending on the specific needs of the department. We'll take an indepth look at three of the plans (including a traditional schedule) beginning on the next page. Before plans are researched and reviewed for appropriateness and adoption by a department, it is best to define expectations and measurable criteria that can be used for objective evaluation. Structuring evaluation criteria in advance, particularly with the benefit of employee input, is one way to assure that the final decision is based on the preferences of existing employees. Below is a sample of some criteria that could be adopted in any department.

Sample Evaluation Criteria[10]

For flexible scheduling plans to be considered for approval and implementation, they must meet, or have the potential to meet, all of the following criteria:

- *Reduce or eliminate staff rotation.*

- *Maintain adequate staffing and acceptable staff-to-patient ratios 7 days a week, 24 hours a day.*

- *Reduce the number of vacant positions.*

- *Reduce overtime, absenteeism, & turnover.*

- *Keep staff at their routine assignment.*

- *Maintain compatibility with established payroll and personnel policies.*

- *Provide for participation by traditional staff in the event that they are willing to help cover for, or temporarily fill, a flexible position.*

- *Ensure fair practice among both flexible and traditional staff members.*

---

[10] Roey Kirk, "Flexible Scheduling," *Nursing Life.* March/April 1983, pages 32-4.

Traditional Schedules

Before examining two new kinds of schedules, let's look at a traditional schedule. This one happens to be for a nutritional services department on the 7-3 shift, but it could be for any department. This department is approved for 8.5 direct FTEs which will accommodate a staffing pattern of 6-7 staff members daily and 5 on weekends. Fixed and nonproductive FTEs have been excluded here to keep the examples simple. This example was calculated and scheduled using the methods discussed earlier in the book.

Department & Shift _NUTRITIONAL SERVICES/7-3_
Payroll Period Ending _JANUARY 16_

Daily Schedule

Name	Position	FTE	Sun Jan 3	Mon Jan 4	Tue Jan 5	Wed Jan 6	Thu Jan 7	Fri Jan 8	Sat Jan 9	Sun Jan 10	Mon Jan 11	Tue Jan 12	Wed Jan 13	Thu Jan 14	Fri Jan 15	Sat Jan 16	Comments
# 1	Registered Dietitian/7-3	1.0		—	—	—	—			—	—	—		—	—		
# 2	Registered Dietitian/7-3	1.0		—	—	—		—	—	—			—	—	—		
# 3	Registered Dietitian/7-3	1.0		—	—		—	—	—	—			—	—	—		
# 4	Registered Dietitian/7-3	1.0		—	—		—	—	—			—	—	—			
# 5	Registered Dietitian/7-3	1.0	—	—						—	—	—	—			—	
# 6	Registered Dietitian/7-3	1.0	—	—						—	—	—			—	—	
# 7	Registered Dietitian/7-3	1.0	—		—	—	—			—	—	—	—				
# 8	Registered Dietitian/7-3	.5	—			—	—								—	—	
# 9	Registered Dietitian/7-3	.5	—		—	—					—				—		
# 10	Registered Dietitian/7-3	.5				—		—	—		—	—					
TOTAL		**8.5**	5	6	6	7	7	7	5	5	6	7	7	6	6	5	

Traditional Scheduling Pattern
(8-hour shifts with every other weekend off)

Description: Ten 8-hour days are worked during a two-week pay period, 40 hours each week. Employees usually have the option of every-other-weekend off (sometimes more or less, depending on the workload of the department). Specific weekdays off each week can be guaranteed (e.g., Monday-Tuesday or Monday & Friday) to employees who work every weekend.

Cost Impact: Employees generally are paid according to a 40 hour per week pay option and begin to accrue pay at time and a half after they have worked 40 hours during one week.

Advantages: It's cost effective in that if an employee works a double shift early in the week, it will be at straight pay; and the time can be taken off later in the week if the employee can be spared. If the employee is needed for the remainder of the week, the hours over 40 hours will be paid at overtime rate.

In departments where employees have a specfic workload to accomplish (and have received administrative approval to be salaried), there can be more flexibility in working hours. For example, an employee who has to stay late an hour to finish his or her work on one day can leave an hour early, if the workload permits, later on in the week. This can help reduce overtime and allows the employee to accomplish the work in a more autonomous, professional manner.

Continuity of care is an important advantage to consider for patient care and service-related departments. Employees are on 3-4 days at a stretch and can provide more continuous, and perhaps even a higher quality of service because of familiarity and repeat experiences with patients.

Disadvantages: It's the generally accepted, traditional norm; and sometimes we think avoiding change is easier.

It's inflexible and not condusive to the life style many individuals want to live. Many healthcare employees don't want to work weekends and are willing to leave their profession because of this requirement. Many others, single parents for example, cannot work 11-7 shifts and are often willing to take a less satisfying, lower paying position, rather than compromise their life style.

It can also be very expensive; because of overtime, absenteeism, turnover costs (hiring, interviewing, orientation), and the unmeasurable cost of dissatisfied employees.

12-Hour Shift Schedules

In the example below, we are looking at the same department, with the same number of approved FTEs; but, in this case, the manager opted to take 2.4 FTEs from the 7-3 shift and 1.2 FTEs from the evening shift to carve out four new positions for dietitians who wanted to work three 12-hour days per week. That's only 36 hours a week, or 0.9 FTE (0.6 from 7-3 and 0.3 from 3-11); but management retained the right to schedule 4 additional hours per week if needed.

Department & Shift _NUTRITIONAL SERVICES/7-3_

Payroll Period Ending _JANUARY 16_

Daily Schedule

Name / Position	FTE	Sun Jan 3	Mon Jan 4	Tue Jan 5	Wed Jan 6	Thu Jan 7	Fri Jan 8	Sat Jan 9	Sun Jan 10	Mon Jan 11	Tue Jan 12	Wed Jan 13	Thu Jan 14	Fri Jan 15	Sat Jan 16	Comments
#1 Registered Dietitian (RD)/7-3	1.0		—	—	—	—			—	—	—	—		—	—	
#2 Registered Dietitian/7-3	1.0		—	—	—	—			—	—	—	—		—	—	
#3 Registered Dietitian/7-3	1.0		—	—	—	—			—	—	—	—		—	—	
#4 Registered Dietitian/7-3	1.0	—		—	—	—		—	—	—	—	—		—		
#5 Registered Dietitian/7-3	1.0	—	—		—	—		—	—		—	—	—	—		
#6 Registered Dietitian/7-3	.5	—					—					—				
#7 Registered Dietitian/7-3	.5	—			—	—			—	—						Sun-on/Sat-off
#8 RD/7A.M.-7P.M	.6	7-7				7-7	7-7				7-7	7-7				7-7	(.9 FTE Total)
#9 RD/7A.M.-7P.M	.6		7-7	7-7			7-7	7-7					7-7	7-7			(.9 FTE Total)
#10 RD/7A.M.-7P.M	.6	7-7				7-7	7-7					7-7	7-7			7-7	(.9 FTE Total)
#11 RD/7A.M.-7P.M	.6		7-7	7-7			7-7	7-7					7-7	7-7			(.9 FTE Total)
TOTAL	**8.4**	**6**	**6**	**6**	**7**	**6**	**6**	**5**	**6**	**6**	**6**	**7**	**6**	**6**	**5**	

Flexible Scheduling Pattern
(12-hour shifts *and* traditional patterns combined)

Description: Six 12-hour days are worked during a two-week pay period, 36 hours each week unless management exercises its option to schedule the extra 4 hours. Some departments actually work 13 hour days to include breaks and to be eligible for 3-11 differential pay after 3 P.M. Your payroll department can advise you in light of your own labor policies and procedures.

Cost Impact: Employees generally are paid according to a 40 hour per week pay option and begin to accrue pay at time and a half after they have worked 40 hours during one week. Most departments schedule staff for a 13-hour day (paid for 12.5 hours) to enable differential pay for the hours after 3:00 P.M. Those who work 7 P.M. to 7 A.M. generally are paid night shift differential for *all* worked hours because the majority of their worked hours are on the night shift.

Advantages: It is a very popular schedule for employees who value their off-duty time, whether it's for personal reasons, education, or the opportunity to work more and earn extra money. It has proved to be an effective recruitment and retention program for the nursing profession.

Because participants are still required to work every other weekend, the department gains an extra 8 hours (per participant) of coverage each weekend, which makes more weekends off a possibility for traditional staff. Some departments pay a weekend differential for the extra 8 hours of weekend time worked (because it's over and above the requirement of two 8-hour days every other weekend) but also offer these employees the first opportunity to be called off in the event they are not needed.

Continuity of care can be both an advantage and a disadvantage. Departments with short interactions with patients indicate that continuity of care is better because there are not so many shift breaks and reports. Other departments, where employees see a patient for several days in a row, feel 12-hour shifts interfere with ongoing continuity.

Disadvantages: When an employee assigned to a 12-hour shift is unexpectedly absent, covering them can be a time-consuming and frustrating task for both the manager and the employee's peers. Adding 12 hours to a 36-hour week can be exhausting for co-workers and expensive for the budget. (On the 40 hour per week pay option, 8 of the additional 12 hours would be at overtime rate.)

12-Hour Weekend Schedules

In the example below, we are looking at the same department and number of approved FTEs; but, in this case, the manager opted to take 2.4 FTEs from the 7-3 shift and 1.2 FTEs from the evening shift to carve out six new positions for dietitians who wanted to work two 12-hour days every weekend. That's 24 hours a week, or 0.6 FTE (0.4 from 7-3 and 0.2 from 3-11). Management retained the right to schedule 8 additional hours per week if needed, at a negotiated time.

Department & Shift *NUTRITIONAL SERVICES/7-3*
Payroll Period Ending *JANUARY 16*

Daily Schedule

Name	Position	FTE	Sun Jan 3	Mon Jan 4	Tue Jan 5	Wed Jan 6	Thu Jan 7	Fri Jan 8	Sat Jan 9	Sun Jan 10	Mon Jan 11	Tue Jan 12	Wed Jan 13	Thu Jan 14	Fri Jan 15	Sat Jan 16	Comments
# 1	Registered Dietitian (RD)/7-3	1.0		—	—	—	—	—		—	—	—	—	—			
# 2	Registered Dietitian/7-3	1.0		—	—	—	—	—		—	—	—	—	—			
# 3	Registered Dietitian/7-3	1.0		—	—	—	—	—		—	—	—	—	—			
# 4	Registered Dietitian/7-3	1.0		—	—	—	—	—		—	—	—	—	—			
# 5	Registered Dietitian/7-3	1.0		—	—	—	—	—		—	—	—	—	—			
# 6	Registered Dietitian/7-3	1.0		—	—	—	—	—		—	—	—	—	—			
# 7	RD/7A.M.-7P.M.	.4	7-7						7-7	7-7						7-7	(.6 FTE Total)
# 8	RD/7A.M.-7P.M.	.4	7-7						7-7	7-7						7-7	(.6 FTE Total)
# 9	RD/7A.M.-7P.M.	.4	7-7						7-7	7-7						7-7	(.6 FTE Total)
# 10	RD/7A.M.-7P.M.	.4	7-7						7-7	7-7						7-7	(.6 FTE Total)
# 11	RD/7A.M.-7P.M.	.4	7-7						7-7	7-7						7-7	(.6 FTE Total)
# 12	RD/7A.M.-7P.M.	.4	7-7						7-7	7-7						7-7	(.6 FTE Total)
TOTAL		8.4	6	6	6	6	6	6	6	6	6	6	6	6	6	6	

Flexible Scheduling Pattern
(Monday - Friday *and* 24-hour weekends combined)

Description: Two 12-hour days are worked every weekend, excluding vacations (which are paid at 40 vacation hours per weekend), unless management opts to schedule an additional shift. In some organizations 7 A.M. to 7 P.M. staff earn evening differential *and* overtime after 8 hours and those working 7 P.M. to 7 A.M. earn night shift differential for all hours worked plus overtime after 8 hours. In other organizations a weekly rate is paid, which, ultimately, increases the participant's hourly salary.

Cost Impact: If employees are not paid at a weekly rate, they generally are paid according to a 8-80 pay option; i.e., they begin to accrue pay at time and a half after they have worked *either* 8 hours in a day, or 80 hours during a two-week period. Thus, each weekend day they work, they are paid at time and a half for the last 4 hours of the shift. Some departments also pay a weekend differential for all 24 hours worked on the weekend, in addition to normal shift differential.[11]

Advantages: As with 12-hour shifts, this is a very popular schedule for employees who value their off-duty time, whether it is for personal reasons, education, or the opportunity to work more and earn extra money. It has proved to be an effective recruitment and retention program for the nursing profession.

It can be cost effective for departments that can use weekend employees during the week for extra coverage, because additional work days (up to 80 hours total) would be paid at straight pay. Also, if staffing requirements go down on the weekend, the manager can offer staff the extra time off.

Disadvantages: Continuity and quality of care become issues because employees are off for five days between their two days on each week. Also, if the entire department staff is split between 24-hour weekend staff and those who are off weekends, there is no overlap and a minimum of communication, which can lead to conflict and error.

It is very expensive and the method of payment can be confusing. Be sure you check with both your personnel and your payroll departments before implementing this program.

When an employee assigned to a 12-hour weekend shift is unexpectedly absent, covering them can be a time-consuming and expensive task for both the manager and the employee's peers. Adding 12 hours to a 40 hour traditional workweek can be exhausting for coworkers and expensive for the budget. (On the 40 hour per week pay option, 8 of the additional 12 hours would be at overtime rate.)

---

[11] This method is a bit complex, but it's preferred over paying employees for hours not worked and allows management a method for paying employees on a traditional schedule bonus pay, should they cover for a 24-hour weekend employee.

Justifying Flexible Scheduling

Justifying the cost of implementing a flexible scheduling program, or even one of the options, obviously is a critical step in the process. Sometimes, individuals responsible for approving such plans have preconceived or negative impressions about the cost effectiveness of these plans; so, it's important to be able to come up with solid information. Be prepared to do your homework.

Start your research activities with the **Satisfaction Questionnaire**, Form 7.1, at the beginning of this section. This will help your employees begin thinking about the things that influence their satisfaction and will also document some feedback. The survey will stimulate natural discussions among staff members, generate a few new ideas, and highlight some specific plans for indepth analysis. It's very important that the manager, who, in his or her own way, is campaigning for approval of flexible scheduling options, has a well-organized and thoughtfully prepared game plan. The research project should be thorough, covering all of the following subject areas: (1) Staff member satisfaction, (2) implementation feasibility, and (3) cost justification.

Staff members can play an important role, particularly when it comes to the area of satisfaction. They can provide their own insights as well as the real scoop from their peers about which plans would be attractive or desirable. Also, most belong to professional organizations or have peer acquaintances outside the organization who can be tapped as resources. Not only do they provide additional opinions and recruitment input but also some might have already experienced implementing flexible scheduling plans at another organization. Learning from others' mistakes and successes saves time and energy, not to mention ego; and, in this case, staff members, patients, and management can all benefit.

Any plan that is considered—whether it's a 24-hour weekend plan or a plan for starting a staffing pool—needs to be looked at carefully to assess the feasibility of implementation. Personnel policies, payroll practices, bylaws, and so forth, not to mention those individuals who seem to be "allergic" to change, all have the potential of circumventing or sabotaging a successful implementation. It's better to find a problem before staff members get their hearts set on a particular plan; and who knows? Maybe you can fix the problem. In one organization management was having a hard time getting approval for a plan that would allow full-time benefits for any employee working 32 hours or more per week because of an ancient personnel policy. After management demonstrated the cost savings of using these employees for extra shifts when needed, as opposed to overtime pay (on the high volume and acuity days) or overstaffing (on the low volume or acuity

Flexible Scheduling Plans:
Justifying Costs

✔ *Collect data to document current costs of:*
  - *Overtime*
  - *Recruitment (advertising, agencies, interviews, hiring)*
  - *Turnover (termination, exit interview, orientation, etc.)*

✔ *Identify dollars saved from unavoidable under-target staffing and use those dollars to fund strategies.*

✔ *Document productivity shift-by-shift to best utilize available staff and cite incidents of under-target staffing.*

✔ *Document other department's work and activities unrelated to clinical role (and the time that is consumed).*

✔ *Track quality assurance problems that can be traced back to under-target staffing.*

days), the increase in benefits costs was dwarfed, the personnel policy was amended, and the plan was implemented.

Cost justification cannot be ignored when doing your homework to justify flexible scheduling options. In the list on the previous page the major areas to consider and document are outlined. If you don't crunch the numbers, someone else will; and, at least if you know what the numbers are, you can plan your offensive. Cost-benefit analysis is a useful tool here because senior managers (with the power to approve plans for implementation) may focus on the additional cost of the new or proposed plan. Flexible scheduling options are usually more expensive in terms of actual salary costs and if you leave it at that, you'll lose. Be creative. Check the **Satisfaction Questionnaires** for some hard data and ask your staff for help in putting a cost on the benefits of implementing flexible schedules.

Consider, for example, the cost associated with dissatisfied employees (e.g., turn-over, low productivity, absenteeism, mistakes, the time it takes for management to counsel them—and there are a lot more). Or, better yet, consider the cost associated with having all budgeted positions filled with satisfied employees (e.g., low overtime, flexibility, time off without panic calls for help with staffing [that's one for management too], and, most importantly, the impact on the quality of the service being delivered by the department). Maybe negotiating a 10 percent improvement in quality, as documented by patient satisfaction surveys, is the key that will unlock the door to approval. Don't hold back if this is an opportunity to improve the quality of care or the service your department provides.

Implementation Strategy

The last subject we'll consider is our plan for implementing approved flexible scheduling options. It is a basic strategic planning format that can be used for any new or revised program, but it is used here in the context of flexible scheduling. Some of the listed activities have been woven through the discussions in this section and every step is important. It is a lot of work; but it is work that your staff members will want to help accomplish, because it will be to their personal benefit and, ultimately, to the benefit of people to whom they provide patient care or a related service.

Flexible Scheduling Implementation Strategy

Step 1: Get top management support to study feasibility & options

2: Educate and involve staff

3: Define/develop:
- program or task force goals
- quality & productivity targets
- organizational constraints

4: Research external market situation

5: Analyze internal considerations (costs, revenues, resource impact)

6: Develop specific objectives

7: Define implementation strategies, including target dates for progress checks and completion

About the Author

Roey Kirk is a noted expert in healthcare management. Using her own experiences from 11 years in both managerial and administrative positions in a 513-bed, community hospital and 5 years as a management consultant, she has developed systems that organize and simplify nursing, clinical, ancillary, and support management functions.

As a consultant, adjunct university instructor of applied management, and seminar leader, Roey Kirk has helped many individuals and organizations make the most of their healthcare management staff. She believes that quality and productivity can exist side by side, and that individual departments can make a positive impact on a hospital's profitability. Using time-tested teaching and training methods, candor, and understanding she shows readers, students, and workshop participants that proactive management skills are not a gift that some are born with, but rather are a set of techniques that can be easily learned, adapted, and used.

Roey Kirk has a bachelor's degree in sociology, a master's degree in management, and is a member of the American College of Healthcare Executives. She has written many articles for healthcare management journals and lectured at many programs nationwide for healthcare managers, administrators, and executives. She has published several books on healthcare management including:

- *Nursing Quality & Productivity: Practical Management Tools (1986)*
- *Nurse Staffing & Budgeting: Practical Management Tools (1986)*
- *Identifying Costs & Pricing Nursing Services: Practical Management Tools (1987)*
- *Healthcare Quality & Productivity: Practical Management Tools (1988)*
- *Healthcare Staffing & Budgeting: Practical Management Tools (1988)*
- *Quality-based Costing, Pricing & Productivity Management for Home Care Organizations (1988)*

She is president and owner of Roey Kirk Associates, healthcare management consultants, in Miami, Florida.